"This book does two remarkable things: it solidly reinforces Christian belief in Jesus as God by gathering the most up-to-date evidence, and it also helpfully reshapes our ways of talking about Jesus as God, in greater conformity with biblical patterns of thought. Lanier doesn't just show that the Bible teaches the deity of Jesus, he shows precisely how the Bible teaches it."

Fred Sanders, Professor of Theology, Torrey Honors Institute, Biola University; author, *The Deep Things of God: How the Trinity Changes Everything*

"'Jesus is Lord' is the fundamental confession of the Christian faith. Writing with the heart of a pastor and the wisdom of a seminary professor, Greg Lanier unfolds the rich Trinitarian framework within which the Old and New Testaments present Jesus as God's divine Son. Anyone who desires to become a more competent reader of the Bible and a more faithful follower of the Lord Jesus Christ will find this book enormously instructive."

Scott R. Swain, author, *The Trinity: An Introduction*; coeditor, *The Oxford Handbook of Reformed Theology*

"Maybe you think you can answer the title of this book with a simple *yes* and move on. But how do you know that Jesus is truly God? Can you articulate that well to others? Why does it matter? What changes about your faith if Jesus isn't truly God? Is Jesus fully God and fully man—even now? In this succinct book, Greg Lanier works through both the Old and New Testaments to present a robust Trinitarian Christology that will equip believers and lead us to further delight in our Lord."

Aimee Byrd, author, *Theological Fitness* and *No Little Women*

"Where would you go in Scripture to prove that Jesus is truly God? In this brief, accessible book, Greg Lanier shows that Christ's divinity doesn't rest on just one or two proof texts. Instead, it's woven into the fabric of the whole New Testament, including the New Testament's use of the Old Testament. *Is Jesus Truly God?* will help you know Jesus and your Bible better. I plan to give it away regularly to church members and to stock it in our church's bookstall."

Bobby Jamieson, Associate Pastor. Capitol Hill Baptist Church; author, *Jesus' Death and He*

T0338955

Is Jesus Truly God?

Is Jesus Truly God?

*How the Bible Teaches the
Divinity of Christ*

Greg Lanier

CROSSWAY®
WHEATON, ILLINOIS

Library of Congress Cataloging-in-Publication Data

Names: Lanier, Gregory R., author.
Title: Is Jesus truly God? : how the Bible teaches the divinity of Christ / Greg Lanier.
Description: Wheaton : Crossway, 2020. | Includes bibliographical references and index.
Identifiers: LCCN 2019025207 (print) | LCCN 2019025208 (ebook) | ISBN 9781433568404 (paperback) | ISBN 9781433568411 (pdf) | ISBN 9781433568428 (mobi) | ISBN 9781433568435 (epub)
Subjects: LCSH: Jesus Christ—Divinity—Biblical teaching. | Trinity—Biblical teaching.
Classification: LCC BT216.3 .L26 2020 (print) | LCC BT216.3 (ebook) | DDC 232/.8—dc23
LC record available at https://lccn.loc.gov/2019025207
LC ebook record available at https://lccn.loc.gov/2019025208

Crossway is a publishing ministry of Good News Publishers.

VP   29 28 27 26 25 24 23 22 21 20
15 14 13 12 11 10 9 8 7 6 5 4 3 2 1

To my wife, Kate,
my true companion in all of life

Contents

Abbreviations

1 En.	1 Enoch
1 Macc.	1 Maccabees
AGJU	Arbeiten zur Geschichte des antiken Judentums und des Urchristentums
AnBib	Analecta Biblica
Ant.	*Jewish Antiquities* (Josephus)
BZNW	Beihefte zur Zeitschrift für die neutestamentliche Wissenschaft
DBTJ	*Detroit Baptist Theological Journal*
De Trin.	*De Trinitate* (Hilary of Poitiers)
Dial.	*Dialogus cum Tryphone* (Justin)
Did.	Didache
Eph.	*To the Ephesians* (Ignatius)
Ezek. Trag.	Ezekiel the Tragedian
Haer.	*Adversus haereses* (Irenaeus)
HBT	*Horizons in Biblical Theology*
JSJSup	Supplements to the Journal for the Study of Judaism

JSNT	*Journal for the Study of the New Testament*
JTS	*Journal of Theological Studies*
Leg.	*Legum Allegoriae* (Philo)
LNTS	Library of New Testament Studies
Marc.	*Adversus Marcionem* (Tertullian)
NovT	*Novum Testamentum*
NSBT	New Studies in Biblical Theology
Paed.	*Paedagogus* (Clement of Alexandria)
Pss. Sol.	Psalms of Solomon
Q (with preceding number)	Qumran texts, i.e., the Dead Sea Scrolls (e.g., 1QS; 4Q174; 4Q252; 11Q5)
Sir.	Sirach/Ecclesiasticus
SJT	*Scottish Journal of Theology*
SNTSMS	Society for New Testament Studies Monograph Series
T. Levi	Testament of Levi
Wis.	Wisdom of Solomon
WUNT	Wissenschaftliche Untersuchungen zum Neuen Testament

Introduction

In a recent interview with an individual seeking to work full-time in a Christian vocation, I asked, "Where would you go in the Bible to show that Jesus Christ is fully divine?" After an uncomfortable pause, the individual ventured in a slightly embarrassed way, "Uh . . . the first chapter of John?" Of course, that is a fine answer, but is there more? This book aims to help equip Christians with a more robust answer to such a question.

Why This Book?

The confession that the true God of all creation is triune—Father, Son, and Holy Spirit—is rooted deeply in the soil of Christian theology. And one of the most debated, and at times perplexing, aspects of this confession is the question "Does Scripture actually teach that Jesus is fully God?"

The early church experienced numerous fights on this front, as Theodotus, Noetus, Arius, Nestorius, and Eutyches (among others) challenged in various ways the full divinity of Jesus Christ. A series of writings and councils spearheaded by a prominent group of early church fathers, ranging from Athanasius to Cyril of Alexandria, defended the traditional doctrine and ruled the competing teachings out of bounds. The key doctrines were crystallized in the Nicene Creed (AD 325) and Chalcedonian Definition (AD 451).

But the debates have not gone away. Outside the church, Jehovah's Witnesses and Mormons reject the Christian teaching that Jesus is fully divine. For instance, the translation of the Bible used by Jehovah's Witnesses (New World Translation) famously renders John 1:1, "The Word was a god," ascribing to Jesus the status of a "god"-like or quasi-angelic being but nothing more. Furthermore, while the Qur'an affirms some true facts about Jesus—such as his birth to Mary and his role as a prophet—Islam holds that the confession of Jesus as the fully divine Son of God is *shirk*, that is, the unforgivable sin of ascribing "partners" to Allah (e.g., Q 'Imran 3:151; Q Nisa' 4:48). And the acid rain of secularism has, for more than two centuries, eroded all possibility of a divine human altogether, instead holding that this doctrine was invented when pagan Greek theology was imported into the church.

Even within the church, Jesus is often taken to be an "ideal human" at best or perhaps simply a good teacher—especially within mainline denominations. But many evangelical Christians are confused or inconsistent as well. A 2018 survey by Ligonier Ministries and LifeWay Research found that nearly 95 percent of self-described evangelical Christians affirm the Trinity, but simultaneously, about 80 percent believe that Jesus Christ is the "first and greatest being created by God."[1] The shocking thing is that these respondents do not appear to realize the stark contradiction in these two positions.

There is thus a clear need for fresh teaching on Christology (i.e., the doctrine of the person and work of Jesus). It could take many shapes: retrieving the teachings of Athanasius, de-

---

1. See "The State of Theology," Ligonier Ministries and LifeWay Research, accessed October 28, 2019, www.thestateoftheology.com.

constructing ancient and modern heresies, summarizing the orthodox teaching from the angle of historical or modern systematic theology, sorting out the complexities of Karl Barth. Each of these paths would be fruitful, but none is the focus of this book.[2]

Instead, I aim to do something even more basic: not only to affirm that, yes, Scripture does indeed teach *that* Jesus Christ is fully God but also to help average Christians understand *how* it does so. It is one thing to know the "right" answer; it is another altogether to understand how the New Testament authors get there—to show their work, so to speak.

Such an endeavor is by no means new. Numerous scholars—particularly among the members of the self-described "early high Christology club" (Richard Bauckham, Martin Hengel, Larry Hurtado, and others)—have recently explored these issues not just in the creeds and church fathers but in the pages of Scripture itself. But the vast majority of their work has focused on one aspect of the issue or one subset of writings (such as Paul's letters), and their output has been largely confined to scholarly monographs and articles. It is high time for the findings to be set forth in a way that reaches a broader audience.[3]

In short, I am arguing that the full *Trinitarian Christology* that is bedrock to Christianity is found throughout the New Testament from the earliest days, is derived from the teachings of Jesus himself, and is rooted in the Old Testament. Put differently, my aim is to help readers discern how the concepts

---

2. In his Simon J. Kistemaker Lectures at Reformed Theological Seminary, Orlando (February 2019), Fred Sanders commented that the "eternal subordination" controversy of 2016–2017 produced much clarification on the person of Christ from a dogmatics perspective but that there is now a need for fresh work proving things more robustly from an exegetical perspective. I hope this small book helps further that goal.

3. Larry W. Hurtado has taken this step in summarizing thirty years of research on early-church worship patterns in his *Honoring the Son: Jesus in Earliest Christian Devotional Practice* (Bellingham, WA: Lexham, 2018). I will cover this topic in chap. 4.

that later coalesce in the creeds are right there in the pages of Scripture from the outset of the Christian church.

But First: The Humanity of the Son

In view of all this, many Christians are surprised to find out that the early church spent just as much time debating whether Jesus Christ was *fully human*, which is rarely a real debate today, as it did debating whether he was fully divine.[4] If the Nicene Creed majors on the question of Jesus's full divinity ("Son of God, begotten of the Father before all worlds . . . very God of very God"), the Chalcedonian Definition majors on his humanity.[5] It affirms that Jesus is "the same perfect in deity and the same perfect in humanity, the same truly God and truly man . . . acknowledged in two natures, unconfusedly, unchangeably, indivisibly, inseparably."[6]

It would be a mistake, thus, to press on in discussing the divinity of Jesus without making clear that the church has historically taught that the two natures—divine and human—cannot be fully separated. Yet the two are also *distinguishable* in various ways ("unconfusedly," per Chalcedon), and there is value in understanding Scripture's teaching on both. It would take another book to iron out the physics of *how* Jesus Christ is fully human and fully divine at the same time. Here I simply survey the New Testament's key affirmations of his humanity before turning the bulk of attention in this book to his divinity.

First, several passages assert that Jesus is human in the fullest possible sense and not just a visible apparition of a deity or angel. Matthew 1:16; Luke 2:6–7; and Galatians 4:4 state that Jesus

---

4. The Docetism controversy—asserting that Jesus only *appeared* human—arose with Serapion (among others) and was refuted in the ecumenical councils.

5. *Trinity Psalter Hymnal* (Willow Grove, PA: Trinity Psalter Hymnal Joint Venture, 2018), 852.

6. Author's own translation from the Greek provided in Jaroslav Pelikan and Valerie Hotchkiss, *Creeds and Confessions of Faith in the Christian Tradition*, vol. 1, *Early Eastern and Medieval* (New Haven, CT: Yale University Press, 2003), 180.

was "born" or "begotten" of a woman. Similarly, John 1:14; 1 Timothy 3:16; and Hebrews 2:14 affirm that Jesus "became," was "manifested in," and "share[d] in" the same kind of "flesh" (Gk. *sarx*) that all humans possess. Throughout the Gospels Jesus eats, walks, sweats, shows emotion, sleeps, and so forth. Even— or perhaps especially—after Jesus's resurrection, the Gospel writers go to great lengths to reiterate that his resurrected body is still a fully human, though transformed, *body*, as seen in John 20:27 (Thomas touches Jesus's scars) and Luke 24:42–43 (Jesus eats a fish). The apostle John emphasizes that he has "seen" and "touched" Jesus (1 John 1:1) and declares that anyone who denies "the coming of Jesus Christ in the flesh" is a deceiver and "antichrist" (2 John 7). Indeed, the full humanity of Jesus is a line in the sand separating true Christianity from unbelief.

Second, the New Testament draws attention to the ways in which Jesus's humanity is not only a true fact but is central to his accomplishing God's redemptive plan. His humanity is essential to his fulfillment of everything expected of the *human* Messiah, or deliverer. I will catalog but a few. Jesus is

- the eschatological prophet like Moses (Acts 3:22)
- a priest in the order of Melchizedek (Heb. 5:10)
- the king like David (Matt. 21:9; Rom. 1:3) who is born from his line (Matt. 1:1–18)
- the anointed one, or Messiah/Christ (Luke 2:11; 9:20; John 20:31)
- the second and greater Adam (Rom. 5:14; 1 Cor. 15:45)
- the servant who would suffer and die vicariously (Acts 8:32–33; 1 Pet. 2:22–23)
- the "root" of Jesse and "star" of Jacob (Rev. 5:5; 22:16— echoing Isa. 11:1 and Num. 24:17, respectively)
- the shepherd of the flock of Israel (John 10:14; Heb. 13:20)

Each is grounded in old covenant promises and comes to fruition in Christ. None of these, strictly speaking, *require* fulfillment by a fully divine person, but they do, often quite explicitly, envision a *human* fulfillment (e.g., shedding of blood, keeping the law in place of Adam). Consequently, these passages highlight how Jesus Christ accomplishes salvation specifically *as a human mediator* (1 Tim. 2:5). Without his full human nature, there is no redemption of humans.

Thus, the question that the rest of this book focuses on is this: How does the New Testament go further and teach that Jesus is specifically a *divine* messianic deliverer? How is he not only a human prophet, priest, king, and mediator but *more than that*—fully God? What I aim to demonstrate is this: the shocking "reveal" of the New Testament that Jesus is not just the Messiah but *more than a Messiah*.[7]

What Is the Goal?

One might at this point interject and ask whether the New Testament ever calls Jesus "God" (Gk. *theos*)[8] and allow that to settle the matter. I will eventually take up that topic (in chap. 6—the short answer is yes). But we cannot start there. While it is an important consideration, calling Jesus *theos* may not necessarily prove anything. *Theos* was typically used in the ancient world for the pantheon, and "divine" or "god" language was regularly employed for human rulers, including Julius Caesar, who was called "divine Julius" (Lat. *divus julius*); Octavian, called "son of a god" (Lat. *divi filius*), and Domitian, called "lord and god" (Lat. *dominus et deus*). Further, in Acts 14:11 the crowds

---

7. To borrow language from Andrew Chester, "The Christ of Paul," in *Redemption and Resistance: The Messianic Hopes of Jews and Christians in Antiquity*, ed. Markus Bockmuehl and James Carleton Paget (London: T&T Clark, 2007), 121.

8. All Greek words are transliterated in lowercase for consistency, even if a word is referring to God. English translations, however, follow normal conventions for capitalizing clear references to God.

in Lystra claim that the "gods" (Gk. *theoi*) have appeared in human form as Barnabas and Paul. Angels are called "gods" in John 10:35. And Paul even calls Satan the *theos* of the present age (2 Cor. 4:4)!

So merely calling Jesus "god" may say little more than what Jehovah's Witnesses—and Arius long before—could affirm.

Other ideas must also be avoided: that Jesus is an angel like Michael or Gabriel or a demigod like Hercules or Achilles, or that he started out as a human and then somehow *became* divine at a later stage. None of these notions capture what early Christians believed. And if that is all we find on the pages of Scripture, then we have a real problem.

Further, we are not looking for something foisted on Jesus long after the fact or for something limited to one or two proof texts (e.g., John 1). If Jesus Christ is truly what the Christian church has confessed—fully man *and fully God* in the way the creeds articulate—then we would expect this belief to be held by Jesus himself and to be saturating the pages of his revealed Word.

So what is the goal of this study? I aim to test whether Scripture actually teaches that Jesus Christ has a real existence from before creation; that he is eternally the second person of the triune God; that there is absolute unity and equality in essence among Father, Son, and Spirit; and that the distinctions in person are not collapsed altogether (such that the Son is absorbed into the Father, or vice versa). Anything else would not be orthodox Christianity.

The goal in the chapters that follow is to demonstrate that a full-orbed divine Christology is taught throughout the entire New Testament, focusing on *how* Scripture does this in six major ways (one per chapter):

1. asserting Jesus's preexistence
2. claiming that Christ is a fully divine "Son"

3. applying the Old Testament in a variety of ways to show that Jesus is fully Israel's God
4. describing early worship offered to Jesus
5. showing the relation of the Son to the Father *and* Holy Spirit
6. directly describing Jesus as *theos* ("God")

1

Preexistence

An Eternally Alive Son

The time-honored science-fiction trilogy *Back to the Future* explores what it would be like for someone to travel back in time and influence past events in such a way that would, in due course, change his own future when he is born. Though mostly pitched as comedy, the films raise intriguing questions about what it means to "exist"—and to shape reality (as when Marty McFly rescues his teenage father from a car wreck)—before you exist. While the movies fall woefully short as analogies to the eternal existence of the Son of God, they do get us thinking in the right direction.

One of the prerequisites for a full doctrine of the divinity of Jesus Christ is that he exists forever in the past. God is, by definition, uncreated. God cannot come into being; he *exists*, from eternity past to eternity future. Yet as we saw in the introduction, Jesus Christ was born as a man. For him to be divine, he somehow must also have had a real, eternal existence even prior to his human birth to Mary. This is typically called *preexistence*: that is, the Son of God was alive and active as a spiritual being before taking on flesh at a particular point in time. He was not just a glimmer in the mind of God, but he was (and is, and always will be) *real*.

The aim of this chapter is to unfold the various ways in which Scripture indeed affirms the Son's real, active, heavenly preexistence within the Godhead. Though such preexistence is often overlooked (perhaps owing to our lack of ability to conceptualize it or to the exclusive focus in some circles on the cross of Christ), this study hopefully puts it more on the layperson's radar.

Heavenly Origin

I begin by examining where Jesus is from.[1] Though the infancy narratives of Matthew and Luke—and Christmas pageants ever since—make the point clear, there was some debate about the birthplace of Jesus during his ministry. Some Jewish crowds questioned whether the Messiah (Gk. *christos*) was to come from Galilee, Bethlehem, or some other place (John 7:40–43).[2] Jesus challenged their preconceived notions, however, when he revealed to various opponents (though cryptically at the time), "I am the living bread that came down from heaven" (6:51), and, "You are from below; I am from above" (8:23).

One does not have to look only at John's Gospel. Paul, writing years before John's Gospel was published, indicates that Jesus's own view about his place of origin was accepted very early by his followers. Paul asks in Romans 10:6, "'Who

---

1. For more details, see Douglas McCready, *He Came Down from Heaven: The Preexistence of Christ and the Christian Faith* (Downers Grove, IL: InterVarsity Press, 2005).
2. As a side note, the reference to Bethlehem in John's Gospel may indicate his familiarity with the birth narratives of Matthew and Luke.

will ascend into heaven?' (that is, to bring Christ down)." This could, in principle, refer to Christ's reign in heaven upon his ascension, but it may refer to his original existence in heaven. A clearer reference is found in a near parallel (Eph. 4:9–10), where Paul describes how Jesus "descended" from *somewhere* to earth, only to reascend to heaven later.

But even if these passages are debatable, Paul states clearly in 1 Corinthians 15:47 that the Son of God "is from heaven." He is not from around here. He existed as a real person, though without a physical body, in the heavenly places. In John 3:31 John the Baptist (or perhaps John the apostle, depending on whether the quotation ends in 3:30 or 3:36) further affirms this by claiming that Jesus is "he who comes from above" and he "who comes from heaven" (cf. 1:15). While it is true that Jesus was physically born in Bethlehem and grew up in Nazareth, he comes from *before* then and from *above* them. He is actually from heaven.

If all this is true, one might expect there to be indications of his heavenly dwelling prior to his physical birth. And that is precisely what is found in the Old Testament.

Let us start with the most famous Old Testament vision of the heavenly court of God: Isaiah 6. The prophet Isaiah sees "the Lord sitting upon a throne," and his "glory" is filling the heavenly temple and the earth (6:1–3). God then speaks directly to Isaiah in 6:9–10, describing the rejection the prophet will face in his ministry. Centuries later, John applies this same text to the rejection Jesus himself faces in his ministry (John 12:40). John then explains that "Isaiah said these things"— that is, Isaiah 6:9–10, which John had just quoted—because he (Isaiah) "saw *his* glory and spoke of *him*" (John 12:41). But to whom are "his" and "him" referring? In the context of the Gospel, the only possibility is Jesus. So what is John saying?

Quite stunningly, the "glory" that Isaiah sees in the heavenly throne room—the radiant and inexpressible manifestation of God himself—is actually *Jesus's* "glory." In other words, John reveals that whomever it was that Isaiah glimpsed in the heavenly throne room was actually the preexistent Son of God in his glory. This is decisive apostolic evidence that the heavenly manifestation of God to an Old Testament prophet was actually the second person of the triune God.

Following Isaiah's cue via John, we might turn to a second major heavenly vision of the Old Testament: Ezekiel 1. In his glimpse into the heavenly throne room, Ezekiel breathlessly tries to capture as best he can what cannot truly be captured in words, ranging from thrones to chariots to angelic beings. He saves the best for last, when he turns his gaze to the expanse above the heavens, where there is "the likeness of a throne" (1:26). Here, at the pinnacle of heaven, is God himself. But notice how Ezekiel describes what he sees: "Seated above the likeness of a throne was a likeness with a human appearance" (1:26). He describes the fiery physical appearance of this human-like figure (1:27) and concludes, "Such was the appearance of the likeness of the glory of the LORD" (1:28). Ezekiel goes to great lengths to make clear that he is not seeing God the Father directly, for no one can see God and live (Ex. 33:20). But what *is* he seeing? The appearance, or the likeness, of the glory of God—which looks like a man! It is God but in human shape, reigning in heaven. Intriguingly, John uses some of these descriptors from Ezekiel 1 to describe Jesus in Revelation (1:15; 2:18), though without directly quoting it. It seems probable that this human-like manifestation of God's glory points, once more, to the preexistent Son.

A final example is found in Daniel 7. It is well known that Jesus regularly refers to himself as "Son of Man" in the New

Testament (~80x). Though there is still much debate about what Jesus means by this enigmatic phrase,[3] the most likely explanation is that he is pointing us to Daniel 7, as becomes clear in Mark 13:26 and 14:62.[4] In another almost indescribable scene, the prophet Daniel recounts a vision of heaven, where "thrones were placed, and the Ancient of Days took his seat," appearing with fire and hair that is white like wool (Dan. 7:9). This, of course, is God himself. But suddenly into the heavenly court appears "one like a son of man," who goes before the Ancient of Days and receives eternal "glory" and an everlasting kingdom (7:13–14).

As history unfolds, this image takes on multiple levels of significance. Jesus uses "Son of Man" to describe his earthly authority (e.g., Mark 2:25–28) and suffering (e.g., 9:31) numerous times during his earthly ministry. "Son of Man" is also a way of capturing Jesus's enthronement at God's right hand immediately after his ascension (Acts 7:56). And it is an eschatological image of Christ's return (Rev. 14:3–14). But there is no reason to think that the scene in Daniel 7, given its multiple layers, was not also, over five hundred years before Christ's birth, a legitimate glimpse of the heavenly preexistence of the Son, particularly when viewed alongside Isaiah 6 and Ezekiel 1.[5]

The plot thickens when one considers an early Jewish translation of Daniel 7:13 into Greek, where this "son of man" does not come "before" the presence of the Ancient of Days (as in

---

3. The most comprehensive recent study is Mogens Müller, *The Expression "Son of Man" and the Development of Christology: A History of Interpretation* (New York: Routledge, 2014).

4. See the robust defense of this position in Michael F. Bird, *Are You the One Who Is to Come? The Historical Jesus and the Messianic Question* (Grand Rapids, MI: Baker Academic, 2009), 79–92.

5. In fact, the Dan. 7 "son of man" is taken precisely as a preexistent figure in 1 En. 48.2–3 ("At that hour that Son of Man was named in the presence of the Lord of Spirits, and his name before the Head of Days. Before the sun and the signs were created, before the stars of the heaven were made, His name was named before the Lord of Spirits"), as well as possibly in 4 Ezra 13:25–26.

Aramaic and other Greek translations) but comes *"as* the Ancient of Days"—suggesting that the two heavenly beings are
somehow identified as the same.[6] Little more might be made
of this if not for how John, in his own apocalyptic vision of
the throne room, takes the attributes of fire and wool-white
hair that Daniel uses for the Ancient of Days and applies them
directly to Jesus (Rev. 1:14), deftly joining their identities in an
impressive though impressionistic way.

When the pieces of Isaiah 6, Ezekiel 1, and Daniel 7 are laid
out on the table—with John as a guide in both his Gospel and
his Apocalypse—a consistent picture starts to emerge from the
puzzle. What these three prophets see, when they have a glimpse
into the heavenlies long before the physical birth of Jesus, is in
some way understood to be the glory of the Son himself alongside the Father. In heaven the Son was already, in eternity past,
the radiant manifestation of the Godhead. *That* is the heavenly
preexistence, the heavenly point of origin, of the incarnate Jesus
Christ. For good reason the prophets all collapsed under the
weight of such a vision (Isa. 6:5; Ezek. 1:28; Dan. 7:15, 28).

"I Have Come"

Every so often a new alien movie comes out. The plot typically
revolves around an alien life-form coming to earth—having
been sent by the mother ship—to accomplish some mission.
The thing that drives the plot is how its *coming* from a different
place of existence brings into sharp relief the massive distinction
between humans and aliens.

Now, I must be careful to emphasize that Jesus Christ is
no alien. (As I established in the introduction, he is emphati-

---

6. This reading is found in most manuscripts of the Old Greek of Daniel; see the tex-
tual apparatus of *Septuaginta: Vetus Testamentum Graecum*, vol. 16.2, *Susanna, Daniel,
Bel et Draco*, ed. Joseph Ziegler and Olivier Munnich, 2nd ed., Societatis Litterarum
Gottingensis (Göttingen: Vandenhoeck & Ruprecht, 1999).

cally understood by himself and all early Christians as truly human.) But if he *is* indeed from somewhere else, not just from Bethlehem—if he is actually from heaven, from "above," as the prophets, apostles, and Jesus himself agree—then one might expect there to be a sense of "coming" from the heavenly realm to the earthly realm. And that is exactly what Scripture conveys.

At various points, the Synoptic Gospels (Matthew, Mark, Luke) state that Jesus has "come" to accomplish something on earth. At first glance, most of these statements seem rather ordinary. Who has not said that he or she has "come" to do something (e.g., "I came to your house to watch the football game")? And no doubt, the verbs that convey "coming" are spoken by Jesus quite a bit. But a few of them merit close inspection. They suggest that Jesus has "come" from somewhere else *to earth*. And that somewhere else, as shown above, can only be heaven. Thus, such statements about Jesus's "coming" from a heavenly place to earth imply his preexistence and, thereby, his distinction from other created humans. Let us look at a few key examples.[7]

First, early in his ministry, Jesus is confronted by an unclean spirit in Capernaum who addresses him as "the Holy One of God" and asks him, "Have you come to destroy us?" (Mark 1:24). A similar encounter takes place with demons in the Gadarene region (Matt. 8:28–29). As spirit beings who apparently once existed in the heavenly realm but are now on earth,[8] the demons instantly recognize who this "Son of God" is. This only makes sense if he was, indeed, preexistent in heaven. And now they ask if he has left heaven and "come" to destroy them on earth "before the time" (Matt. 8:29).

7. See the extensive treatment of the evidence by Simon J. Gathercole, *The Preexistent Son: Recovering the Christologies of Matthew, Mark, and Luke* (Grand Rapids, MI: Eerdmans, 2006).

8. As may be deduced from, say, Deut. 32:17; 2 Cor. 11:13–15; Rev. 12:7–9 (though the evidence is sparse).

Second, Jesus makes one of his classically difficult statements in Luke 12:49–51 when he asserts, "I came to cast fire on the earth. . . . Do you think that I have come to give peace on earth?" There is much debate about what "fire" means and why Jesus speaks so harshly. For the present purposes, the key is that Jesus is self-aware that he has "come" specifically to "earth" to accomplish judgment. It would make little sense for the average Joe to say that he has "come" to bring fire or peace to earth *if he is from earth*—what would that even mean? The most logical way of taking this statement is that Jesus is attesting that he has "come" from *outside the realm of earth* to do something *on the earth*. Moreover, if the "fire" is one of judgment, then the closest parallels to this idea are found in passages where *God* sends fire from heaven to earth (e.g., Gen. 19:24; 2 Kings 1:10, 12–14; 1 Chron. 21:26; Job 1:16; Luke 9:54; Rev. 20:9).

Third, Jesus summarizes the entirety of his earthly ministry when he claims, "The Son of Man came not to be served but to serve, and to give his life as a ransom for many" (Mark 10:45). While many issues pertaining to atonement hinge on this verse, I focus here on the use of "come." Jesus is clearly not saying he has "come" to any specific location (like Capernaum, Nazareth, or Jerusalem), for what he has in mind extends to all mankind in some way. And, moreover, the scope of what he is doing is not to "teach a bit in Galilee" or to "do some miracles in Bethany" but to provide salvation that is world encompassing. Thus, it is best to take this verse as indicating that the entire mission of the Son is to "come" from somewhere, *to earth*, in the flesh, to offer his life as a ransom.

In these instances, Scripture records a clear statement from Jesus that he has "come" to accomplish something, but that something presupposes either a heaven-earth distinction (as in the first two examples) or a whole-earth scope (as in the third). These "I have come to do X" statements amount to more than what any ordinary human, or even prophetic figure, could say. They suggest that Jesus is fully conscious that he "comes" from beyond the human realm. In fact, the "I have come" statements of Jesus sound very much like what angels say when they leave heaven and "come" to earth for some specific purpose (e.g., 1 Kings 22:19–22; Dan. 9:22–23; 10:13–14; Luke 1:19).

If Jesus has self-awareness of "coming" from somewhere else into the earthly realm, do his earliest followers share that awareness? Yes, several examples indicate that they do. In one of his earliest letters, Paul states that "when the fullness of time had come, God sent forth his Son, born of woman" (Gal. 4:4). The Son existed chronologically before the "fullness of time" and then was "sent forth" to be born of a woman. This is re-iterated in Romans 8:3, where Paul attests to God's "sending his own Son in the likeness of sinful flesh." The person we now know as Jesus did not start to exist when he was born in the flesh, but he was *already the Son in his preexistence*, and then he was "sent" in the flesh. Paul even passes on an early Christian "trustworthy saying" about this movement from outside the world into it, recording that "Christ Jesus came into the world" (1 Tim. 1:15). Furthermore, John twice states that God "sent" his Son "into the world" (John 3:17; 1 John 4:9), and Hebrews 10:5 speaks of "when Christ came into the world." As with Paul, both John and the author of Hebrews attest that the Son, or the Christ, was "sent" or "came" into the world, implying that he originated from outside it.

In short, both Jesus and the apostolic circle offer a few ways of thinking about his preexistence. Temporally, he existed in eternity past and then "came" at a point in time. Location-ally, he existed in heaven before "coming" or being "sent" to earth. Existentially, he was a true spiritual person as "Son" before taking on flesh as a human. This preexistent, heavenly origin of Jesus Christ makes him entirely different from any other human and creates the space for him to be an eternally uncreated God—though I add more details in the following chapters to develop this argument further.

Active Role in the Life of Israel

If, as the preceding two sections have suggested, the Son of God already existed eternally in the heavenly realm before "coming" or being "sent" to the earthly realm, another question arises. What was he doing back then? For, recall, we are exploring not just a theoretical kind of preexistence—like an idea in God's head—but a *real* preexistence. Granted, as limited humans, we lack the mental horsepower to fully understand this. But if Christ did have a real preexistence and was not just a glimmer in the imagination of God, then one would expect him to be active in the period before his birth. Strikingly, Scripture does indeed show signs of the Son's preexistent activity.

I begin by looking at how Jesus himself provides the key to seeing how he was present and active during the Old Testament era. Then I probe other examples where the curtain is pulled back to reveal a glimpse of the Son's work centuries before his birth to Mary.

The Son in the Psalms

A great launching point is how Jesus reads himself into Psalm 110 in Mark 12:35–37.[9] In this influential psalm, David writes,

---

9. For more extensive analysis on this use of Psalm 110 (and similar examples)—often dubbed "prosopological exegesis"—see Matthew W. Bates, *The Birth of the Trinity: Jesus, God, and Spirit in New Testament and Early Christian Interpretations of the Old Testament* (Oxford: Oxford University Press, 2015); Matthew Scott, *The Hermeneutics*

YHWH said to my *Adon*,
"Sit at my right hand." (Ps. 110:1, my trans.)

Examining the psalm closely, we find that there are three persons in the mix: YHWH (usually displayed in English translations as "LORD," in small caps), who is speaking; *Adoni* (usually translated "my Lord"), to whom YHWH is speaking; and David, who is recording this speech and referring to *Adon* as "my." In other words, David is writing down something that YHWH says to his (i.e., David's) *Adon*. Even in the ancient context of the psalm itself, this is rather striking. But its beauty is multiplied when Jesus reveals its true sense.

In a key moment when he turns the tables on the religious opponents who have perpetually picked fights with him about scriptural matters, Jesus asks,

How can the scribes say that the Messiah/*christos* is the son of David? David himself, in the Holy Spirit, declared,

"The Lord said to my Lord,
'Sit at my right hand.'" . . .

David himself calls him "Lord." So how is he his son? (Mark 12:35–37, my trans.)

This is a bit complex, so let us break it down.

Jesus brings up the common Jewish belief that the Messiah/*christos* is the "son of David."[10] He then goes back to Psalm 110 and points out that David refers to this Messiah figure,

of Christological Psalmody in Paul: An Intertextual Enquiry, SNTSMS 158 (Cambridge: Cambridge University Press, 2014); Aquila H. I. Lee, *From Messiah to Preexistent Son: Jesus' Self-Consciousness and Early Christian Exegesis of Messianic Psalms*, WUNT, 2nd ser., vol. 192 (Tübingen: Mohr Siebeck, 2005). Irenaeus, among others, supports this take on Psalm 110 (*Haer.* 3.6.1).

10. As expressed in, say, 2 Sam. 7:12–13 and elaborated in intertestamental writings such as Pss. Sol. 17.4–46; 4Q174; 4Q252.

who is enthroned at God's right hand, as "my Lord"—that is, *Adoni*, discussed above. He concludes with an open-ended question: If David refers to this person as "my Lord," how can he also be his "son"? Upon inspection, it becomes clear that Jesus is saying that the very same person is simultaneously (1) the "son of David," (2) the Messiah/*christos*, and (3) the "my Lord" (*Adoni*) that David is describing in Psalm 110:1. And while Jesus leaves his audience hanging at this point, those with ears to hear quickly realize that Jesus is identifying *himself* as that very person, fitting all three descriptions.

In other words, here is how Jesus reads Psalm 110: David, who was "in the Holy Spirit," has recorded a conversation between YHWH and someone David calls "my Lord" (*Adoni*), whom Jesus now reveals to be the "son of David" and "Messiah/*christos*"—namely, himself. And all this is roughly a millennium before Jesus comes. The whole scene being described in Psalm 110 is now unveiled to be fantastically Trinitarian: the Spirit reveals that the Father (YHWH) addresses the Son (David's Lord/*Adon*) in his heavenly preexistence and seats him at his right hand to rule over all things. *When* this happens and *how* to work out all the details are beyond the present scope. What matters is that Jesus directly attests that he, as the preincarnate Son of the Father, is the one being addressed by YHWH in Psalm 110, long before his human birth.[11]

This psalm does not simply point to or anticipate or prefigure the coming of the Son; *it is profoundly about him from*

---

11. Psalm 110:1 is also cited elsewhere in the New Testament with reference to the ascension of Jesus after his resurrection (e.g., Acts 2:34–35). Thus, it appears that Jesus and the apostolic authors find multiple ways of interpreting the verse: *prior* to his death and resurrection, Jesus points us backward to David's day and, thereby, his preincarnate existence (in Mark 12); *after* the resurrection, other New Testament authors point forward to the ascension. This dual reading of Ps. 110 is consistent with the notion that Christ comes from his heavenly throne (in his incarnation) and, in a sense, is "re"-enthroned when he returns to heaven (after fulfilling his earthly ministry).

the outset. It is a record of the Father and the preexistent Son talking to one another in the heavenly throne room in times past. That is truly stunning. Moreover, in the ancient Greek translation of Psalm 110, God is described as addressing these words to the Son/*Adoni*/Lord figure:

> From the womb, before the morning star,
> I have begotten you. (Ps. 110:3, my trans.)

This, too, fits with how the psalm points to the eternal "begetting" of the preexistent Son.

This marvelous disclosure by Jesus that he is being directly addressed in this psalm influences various New Testament authors. Periodically in the New Testament, Jesus, not David or someone else, is revealed to be the active participant in different psalms:

- Acts 2:25–35: Peter reveals that in Psalms 16 and 110, "David [spoke] concerning him," that is, Jesus—not himself—when he spoke about burial and ascension.
- Acts 13:33–37: Paul argues (as with Peter) that Psalms 2 and 16 were not really about David (who "fell asleep . . . and saw corruption") but about Jesus.
- Romans 15:2–3: Paul argues that Psalm 69 was speaking about Christ's self-humbling.
- Hebrews 2:11–12: The author describes the words of Psalm 22 as something Jesus speaks.

These passages do not necessarily convey Christ's preexistence, but they do express how some psalms as originally given had a longer-term, Christological horizon in view.

But one more example *does* evoke preexistence, as the closest parallel to Jesus's teaching on Psalm 110. In Hebrews 1:8–9, the author recounts how God is speaking in the Psalms and observes that "to the Son, he says, 'Your throne . . . ,'" quoting Psalm 45:6–7 (my trans.).[12] According to Hebrews, God is speaking to (Gk. *pros*) a "you" in Psalm 45, and that "you" is the Son. The likelihood that Hebrews is indeed treating Psalm 45 in the same way that Jesus treated Psalm 110—namely, as revealing a conversation between the Father and the preexistent Son about his heavenly throne—increases when we arrive at the end of the chapter (Heb. 1:13). The author concludes his series of Old Testament quotations precisely with Psalm 110, which God "said" not to the angels but to his Son.

The Son in Ancient Israel

To summarize the point so far, I have attempted to show that Jesus and the author of Hebrews appear to treat at least some psalms as Spirit-inspired records of prior conversations between the Father and Son in heaven, long before the Son's birth on earth. But if Israelites like David were in some way aware of such an intrinsic plurality in the one true God (though how much they humanly understood is unclear), is there any evidence that the second person of this Godhead was actually involved in their lives even back then? Perhaps surprisingly, the answer is yes. The New Testament authors look back and give a few examples of the preexistent Son at work in the life of Israel.

When the Israelites were in the wilderness, God provided water from a rock, beginning at Exodus 17:6 and ending at Numbers 20:8–11 (cf. Deut. 8:15; Neh. 9:15). But Paul reveals that, in some way that remains mysterious to us, "the Rock was Christ" (1 Cor. 10:4). Paul goes on to say that, when the Israel-

---

12. "To the son" better captures the force of the Greek *pros ton huion* than, say, the ESV's "of the son."

ites grumbled against Moses as they circumnavigated the land of Edom—resulting in God's sending serpents among them (Num. 21:5–6)—they had actually "put Christ to the test" (1 Cor. 10:9). Paul does not work out the mechanics for the reader. He simply implies that the preexistent Son was actually present with Israel during the ups and downs of their wilderness sojourn, sustaining them and even being the target of their grumbling.

Jude pushes the chronology further back in time. In an oft-overlooked passage, he most likely writes, "I want to remind you . . . that Jesus, who saved a people out of the land of Egypt, afterward destroyed those who did not believe" (Jude 5).[13] The implications are quite astounding. Here the half brother of the earthly Jesus says that this same Jesus was active as a real divine person who rescued his people in the exodus, some 1,500 years before his physical birth.

Such a reading of Jude 5 raises another intriguing possibility, especially when viewed in tandem with how Paul parallels "angel of God" with Christ (Gal. 4:14). The church has long debated whether and when the enigmatic "angel of the LORD" (or similar figures) is actually a preincarnate appearance of the Son of God. According to Moses's own reckoning, it is precisely such an angel who led the people out of Egypt and guided them through the wilderness (Ex. 14:19; 23:20; 32:34; etc.). Hence, Jude 5 indicates that "the angel of the LORD"— at least in these instances—is apparently *the same entity as the preexistent Son of God.*

---

13. I say "most likely" because this section of Jude in the Greek is very thorny. There are over thirty textual variations for Jude 5 in the known Greek manuscripts, according to Barbara Aland et al., *Novum Testamentum Graecum: Editio Critica Maior,* vol. 4.1, *Die Katholischen Briefe,* 2nd ed. (Stuttgart: Deutsche Bibelgesellschaft, 2013). Many manuscripts read that "God" led this exodus from Egypt; many others say that it is the "Lord" who did so. But based on the latest research, the most likely initial version, written by Jude, is that it is "Jesus" who led this exodus. The main scholarly Greek edition was recently updated to accept this reading instead of "Lord," though many English translations were already doing so.

Other candidates that are often debated as possible Old Testament appearances of Christ ("Christophanies") include the following:

- the three angelic "men" of Genesis 18 (one of whom is God himself)
- the angelic "man" who wrestles with Jacob in Genesis 32
- the "angel of the LORD" who appears to Moses in the burning bush in Exodus 3
- the angelic "man" who commands the armies of God in Joshua 5
- the "angel of the LORD" who appears as a "man of God" to Manoah's wife in Judges 13
- the mysterious fourth "man" who looks like a "son of the gods" in the furnace of Daniel 3
- the angelic judge in Zechariah 3

In such passages we have angelic figures who represent the Lord and are often partially equated with him but yet remain distinct in some way. For good reason, then, the church has long grappled with whether such scenes picture the active role of the Son before his incarnation.[14]

The cumulative force of these examples is this: the Son of God was present and active in the life of Israel even before his human birth. This is precisely what one would expect if he was, indeed, fully divine and dwelling in the heavenly places before all time, prior to his being "sent" into the world. And this evidence may shed some light on what Jesus was getting at

---

14. See, for instance, Justin, *Dial.* 58–61; Irenaeus, *Haer.* 3.6.1–2; Tertullian, *Marc.* 3.9; Hilary of Poitiers, *De Trin.* 4.23–24. More recent studies of the role of angels in the formation of early Christology include Peter Carrell, *Jesus and the Angels: Angelology and the Christology of the Apocalypse of John*, SNTSMS 95 (Cambridge: Cambridge University Press, 2005); Charles A. Gieschen, *Angelomorphic Christology: Antecedents and Early Evidence*, AGJU 42 (Leiden: Brill, 1998). Keep in mind that many studies of "angelomorphic Christology" do not fall in line with orthodox Trinitarianism.

when he declared, "Abraham . . . saw [my day] and was glad" (John 8:56).

Explicit Statements of the Son's Preexistence

I wrap up with some of the most direct statements of the preexistence of the Son in the New Testament. I avoided beginning here because laying the foundation using other passages helps show that these statements are not outliers but that they simply corroborate the other evidence.

First, Paul states plainly that Jesus Christ is "before all things" (Col. 1:17), most likely using the Greek preposition *pro* in a temporal sense. From the perspective of time, the Son is antecedent to the creation of all things.

Second, Paul draws on what is likely an early Christian confession when he affirms that Christ "was manifested in the flesh" (1 Tim. 3:16). While previously I focused on the "flesh" part of this verse, here I want to focus on the "manifested" part. For Paul—and early Christians—to make this confession, they had to presuppose that Christ existed beforehand. Otherwise, the use of "manifested" would make no sense. It is not a verb that is used for something that comes into being from scratch; it is used for something that already exists but is more fully disclosed. Thus, this passage holds that the Son already existed, and *then* he was manifested or unveiled in the flesh. This conviction is voiced even more clearly by Peter, when he describes how Christ "was foreknown before the foundation of the world but was made manifest in the last times" (1 Pet. 1:20). The Son existed before the creation of the world, but at a point in time, he was "manifested" (the same verb as above) on earth.

Third, Paul writes how Christ "was rich, yet for your sake he became poor" (2 Cor. 8:9). At first glance this may seem to be simply making a statement about Jesus's economic status.

But note that Jesus was never "rich" in his earthly life, nor did his standard of living change. He was born into relative poverty,[15] and throughout his adulthood he was clearly not materially "rich." So when was he "rich," according to Paul? The likeliest explanation, when this passage is compared with others in Paul's letters, is that Paul is alluding to the riches the Son had in his preexistent glory, and so his becoming "poor" refers to his earthly incarnation and suffering.

Finally, consider the clearest and most stunning statements by Jesus himself: "I have come down from heaven" (John 6:38); "Before Abraham was, I am" (8:58); and "Father, glorify me in your own presence with the glory that I had with you before the world existed" (17:5). Stronger affirmations of a real, heavenly existence of Jesus before Abraham—yes, even before the creation of the world—could scarcely be found.

Summary

The thrust of this chapter has been to sketch how the Old and New Testaments affirm that the Son of God existed in eternity past before he took on flesh and was placed in the manger in Bethlehem. His *real* point of origin is the heavenly places, which some Old Testament prophets glimpsed. From heaven he "came," having been sent from above to the world to accomplish his task. But even before he "came," he was active in the life of Israel, though often in the shadows.

What is perhaps most impressive is that these claims about the preexistence of the Son come from so many angles across the New Testament. Some passages are quite direct, while others are more subtle. Some authors, like Paul, discuss it more frequently than others, but nearly every New Testament author

---

15. For instance, Luke 2:24 records how Joseph and Mary apparently offered two birds in Jerusalem upon Jesus's birth, which is an accommodation for those who are poor in Lev. 12:8.

deals with the idea in some way. But standing as the fountainhead of it all, as far as the evidence suggests, is Jesus himself. While Jesus did not wear a name tag that read, "I am the pretemporal and preearthly Son of God from heaven," he came pretty close, using the scriptural concepts of his own day. It is unsurprising, then, that we see his followers reflect their teacher's self-awareness in so many ways.

So What?

The preexistence of the Son is such an important but often overlooked doctrine that a moment's reflection on the "so what" is merited.

Many Christians approach the Old Testament with only two tools: prophetic fulfillment ("what was predicted back then has come to pass in Jesus") and typology ("this person/place/thing in ancient Israel was playing a redemptive function that culminates in Jesus"). While both tools are valid and powerful, they tend to impose a gap between the era of Israel and the incarnation of Christ—essentially ignoring his preexistence.

The material of this chapter might help the church recover the instinct of not just seeing the Old Testament as something that *pointed forward* to the Son of God (which it does) but seeing the Son *at work even back then*. This should, in turn, affect how we preach and teach Christ from all Scripture, giving us more tools to work with than simply straining to find the cross in every nook and cranny of the Old Testament.

2

God the Son

A Unique Father-Son Relation

Across languages, family terms are often stretched beyond actual bloodlines. A close friend in Spanish may be styled *mi hermano* ("my brother"). Or in German one's home country may be termed the *Vater Staat* ("father state") or the *Mutterland* ("motherland"). But most people realize (even subconsciously) when a family term is being used for a literal or adoptive relationship and when it is being extended metaphorically. And the difference is important.

For instance, a famous photo portrays John F. Kennedy Jr. playing on the floor of the Oval Office in the White House when his father was serving as president of the United States. Junior had that kind of intimate access to the most powerful political figure of that era because he was the true son of the president, because JFK was his father. Compare this with, say, the innumerable small business names that end with "and

Sons." The other people included in the "and" are not always biological or adoptive "sons" but may simply be employees or friends of the titular figure. They are *designated* "sons" because that gives a certain ring to the function they play in the business. But they do not necessarily share in the kind of thing that makes a true father-son relationship what it is.

This flexibility of "father" and "son" becomes important when one turns attention to how these words are used for the Godhead in Scripture. An essential way by which the second person of the triune God is known is "Son," and likewise "Father" for the first person of the Trinity. These terms are intrinsic to how God has revealed himself. But what does "Son" or "Son of God" actually mean in Scripture?

The Nicene Creed (AD 325) uses Father-Son terminology to convey Jesus's full divinity: "Son of God, begotten from the Father before all ages, God of God."[1] That is, "Son of God" means Jesus is of the same essence or substance—the same *kind of existence*—as the divine Father and has been so from eternity past. But New Testament scholars have, for many years, argued that such a meaning of "Son" was foisted onto the term later. Rather, they claim that the New Testament uses "Son of God" simply as a functional title for a human messianic king, not the divinely begotten Son in the sense of the creeds.[2] The theological difference is substantial.

So who is right? I aim to demonstrate in this chapter that, while the latter view contains much truth, the former view—that "Son of God" can also express Jesus's divine begetting by the Fa-

---

1. *Trinity Psalter Hymnal* (Willow Grove, PA: Trinity Psalter Hymnal Joint Venture, 2018), 852.
2. The most thorough treatments along these lines in recent years are Michael Peppard, *The Son of God in the Roman World: Divine Sonship in Its Social and Political Context* (Oxford: Oxford University Press, 2011); Adela Yarbro Collins and John J. Collins, *King and Messiah as Son of God: Divine, Human, and Angelic Messianic Figures in Biblical and Related Literature* (Grand Rapids, MI: Eerdmans, 2008).

ther—is likewise grounded in Scripture. If so, then at Nicaea the divine meaning of "Son" was not invented but elaborated on.

"Son of God" Can Be a Flexible Label

Among the significant findings brought to light by the Rosetta Stone (ca. 200 BC) is the portion that designates King Ptolemy as "son of Ra," where Ra is the sun god. But this is actually not that unusual for the ancient world. Various people groups regularly styled their monarchs "sons" of the gods in their pantheons. This continued into the Greco-Roman era; recall from chapter 1 that Octavian (Augustus) was styled "son of a god." The mere use of royal "son" language, however, does not imply that these kings were seen to be literally divine like Ra or Zeus or whomever—not even in Egypt, where the exalted status of various pharaohs was quite pronounced. Rather, the sense was that these kings derived their authority and power from the deity in a very special way, which is captured by use of the label "son."

Similar language occurs in the Old Testament. For instance, God tells David that his royal successor "shall be to me a son" (2 Sam. 7:14; 1 Chron. 17:13), which is echoed in Psalms 2:7 and 89:26. Such royal sonship in the life of Israel is an extension of how God declares the nation itself to be his "firstborn son" (Ex. 4:22–23) and he their "father" (Jer. 31:9). Thus, the king of Israel is "son" of God as the representative of all the Israelites, who are, likewise, "sons" of God.[3] By itself, this use of sonship language for Israel or Israel's king need not imply that David or Solomon or anyone else is divine; it simply reflects a broader pattern of royal "son" language common for the period.

As Judaism developed, such "son of God" language was sometimes taken to be explicitly messianic. For instance, one of the Dead Sea Scrolls elaborates on 2 Samuel 7:14 as follows:

---

3. See similar uses of "sons of God" for righteous Israelites in Wis. 2:12–20; 5:1–5.

"'He will be to me a son.' This is the Sprout of David who will stand forth . . . in the end of days" (4Q174); this "Sprout" is elsewhere called "the Messiah" in other scrolls (e.g., 4Q252). Moreover, another scroll denotes an eschatological king as "Son of God and Son of the Most High" (4Q246).

Based on these patterns in the ancient world and the Old Testament itself, there is good reason to think that some Jews in Jesus's day would understand "Son of God" not to imply full divinity but to be a kind of messianic epithet or label. During Jesus's trial, for instance, the high priest demands, "Tell us if you are the Messiah/*christos*, the Son of God" (Matt. 26:63, my trans.)—paralleling the terms "Messiah" and "Son of God." Earlier, Nathanael, Peter, and Martha make the same parallel by confessing, respectively, "You are the Son of God! You are the King of Israel!" (John 1:49); "You are the Messiah/*christos*, the Son of the living God" (Matt. 16:16, my trans.); and "You are the Messiah/*christos*, the Son of God" (John 11:27, my trans.). And after Jesus is crucified, based (in part) on the accusation that he claimed to be "King of the Jews," the centurion guarding his body remarks, "Surely this was son of God" (Matt. 27:54, my trans.),[4] perhaps using the term in the political way familiar to him as a Roman.

A clear pattern emerges: sometimes in the New Testament, "Son of God" appears to be more or less interchangeable with "king" or "Messiah/*christos*." This is no doubt significant, showing how Jesus fulfills the messianic promises of the Old Testament. But such use does not necessarily imply full (ontological) divinity.

But what about when the disciples fall prostrate before Jesus in the boat, acclaiming him to be "Son of God" (Matt. 14:33)

---

4. Many translations place "the" or "a" before "son of God" here, but there is no article in the Greek. It is best, then, to leave it out to capture the ambiguity.

months *before* they confess him to be "Messiah" (Matt. 16:16)? What about Satan and the demons who, with supernatural insight, address Jesus as "Son of God" (Mark 3:11; Luke 4:3, 9)? Such examples prompt us to explore whether "Son" and "Father" language in the New Testament can extend beyond royal messiahship into the realm of the divine.

Jesus Expresses His Unique Sonship

A good place to start is with the statements of Jesus himself. Did he use sonship language only for a kind of messianic self-awareness, or is there more?

The first piece of evidence can be found in the poignant scene in the garden, where Jesus, in a moment of anguish that anticipates the even greater one to come, calls out to "Abba, Father" (Mark 14:36). This is a unique occurrence in the Gospels, where Jesus addresses God with the Semitic word *abba* (transliterated into Greek), to which is added the Greek word *patēr*. It is often taught that Abba means something like "Daddy" in colloquial English, as something a child would say. Most likely this is an exaggeration.[5] Whether Mark's transliterated Greek word reflects an Aramaic form (like *'abbā*) or a Hebrew form (like *'ābi*), either way it is best understood to be an ordinary word for one's own "father," regardless of who is uttering it. (The presence of the normal Greek "father" alongside it would confirm this.)

That said, the intimacy of this scene should not be downplayed altogether. In a moment of tearful foreboding, Jesus cries out specifically to his Abba for deliverance. He does not plead to "God" or "Most High" or "Lord" or "Savior"—all of which were options (cf. Gk. *Elōi*, "My God," in Mark 15:34). Rather, he implores the one who stands—in the moment of

---

5. See James Barr, "'Abbā Isn't 'Daddy,'" *JTS* 39, no. 1 (1988): 28–47.

crisis—as *relationally* "Father" to him. He appeals to Abba to draw near to him and do his will, even if it requires the life of the Son. While the coloring of Abba is not quite "Daddy," its use in addressing God with such profound closeness *is* something that lacks much precedent in early Judaism. An ordinary Jew in Jesus's day would rarely presume to address the God of the universe in such a familiar way.

Jesus also speaks to his followers about "my Father" (Matt. 26:53; Luke 22:29; 24:49; John 5:17; 6:40; 8:19). Given that Jesus elsewhere describes God corporately as "our Father" (Matt. 6:9), there is a special significance to this personal "my." Even as a boy, Jesus is aware that his *true* Father is not Joseph on earth; rather, "my Father" is God himself (Luke 2:49). Interestingly, this use of "*my* Father" to refer to God is something only Jesus does in the New Testament; even the apostles avoid referring to God as "my Father" (preferring "our," as in Rom. 1:7; 1 Cor. 1:3; 2 Cor 1:2; etc.). And in the Old Testament, the only such occurrences of the phrase are spoken by God himself as a kind of future promise (Ps. 89:26) or hypothetical scenario (Jer. 3:19). So its use by Jesus is almost unparalleled.

Moreover, in several instances Jesus goes one step further and denotes his true Father as "my Father *in heaven*," indicating that he stands in a sonship relation not to someone "below" but to someone "above" (Matt. 7:21; 10:32; 12:50; 16:17; 18:19). And finally, Jesus refers to himself as "the Son" and to God as specifically "the Father" (Mark 13:32).

Throughout his earthly ministry, Jesus suggests that he stands in a unique relation to the Father, who is specifically "his." Their identities define one another: the heavenly Father is specifically *his Father*, and Jesus is specifically *the Son* of that Father. It is not surprising, then, that in John's apocalyptic vision, the exalted Jesus once again refers to "my Father" in a unique and exclusive way (Rev. 2:27; 3:21).

The Father Addresses the Son

If Jesus affirms that he is uniquely the Son, does the Father return the favor, so to speak? At various points the Father indeed does.

First, in Matthew's birth account, the angel commands Joseph to escape Herod's murderous plot by fleeing to Egypt with Mary and young Jesus. Sometime later, it is safe enough for them to return. Matthew intriguingly applies Hosea 11:1 to that situation (Matt. 2:14–15): namely, when God says, "Out of Egypt I called my son," he is ultimately referring to *this Son*, the young child of Mary. This maneuver by Matthew is quite complex, but what is clear is this: via the mouth of Hosea's ancient prophecy, God the Father declares the young boy Jesus to be, in a profound sense, "my Son."[6]

Second, God speaks again when Jesus begins his earthly ministry. As many Jews flock to John the Baptist near the Jordan River to be baptized, Jesus follows suit. Luke records that while Jesus is addressing his Father in prayer, the Father replies audibly from heaven, "You are my beloved Son; with you I am well pleased" (Luke 3:22). Though this baptism scene does indeed mark Jesus as the anointed deliverer at the inauguration of his ministry (echoing Ps. 2), this strong paternal language bursting forth from heaven—"my beloved Son"—seems to point beyond the horizon of a human, earthly deliverer.

---

6. This use of Hos. 11:1 by Matthew is somewhat notorious in modern New Testament studies, particularly for those who believe Matthew must be (mis)using the passage solely as a *messianic* prophecy—whereas Hos. 11 is not really messianic. But this tension is easily resolved when one realizes that that is not necessarily what Matthew is doing. Rather, he is portraying Jesus as the embodiment or representative of Israel, and in that sense he is the true "son" of Hos. 11. This theme continues as Jesus joins repentant Jews in receiving John's baptism, spends forty days in the wilderness, ascends the mountain to preach the law of God, and so on.

Finally, this dialogue reoccurs at the transfiguration of Jesus. As Peter, James, and John catch an eyewitness glimpse of Jesus's future glory (recalled in 2 Pet. 1:16–18), the voice of the Father once again bursts forth. About the transfigured one he declares, "This is my beloved Son; listen to him" (Mark 9:7). Once again, from the Father's perspective, Jesus Christ is specifically *his* "Son."

In short, the way the Father addresses Jesus as "Son" is a distinct and special indicator of their relation to one another— so much so that the author of Hebrews emphasizes that God never addresses the angels but only Jesus himself as "Son" (Heb. 1:5).

The Oneness of Father and Son

The apex of these declarations of how the Son and Father uniquely share this strong relational bond is found in the Gospel of John.

Jesus speaks of how, in eternity past, he learned from the Father what he would, upon his coming to earth, proclaim: "I declare to the world what I have heard from him. . . . [I] speak just as the Father taught me. . . . I speak of what I have seen with my Father" (John 8:26, 28, 38). While the Father's teaching of the Son and the Son's hearing could, in theory, refer to Jesus's prayer life and study of the Torah, the "seen with" almost by necessity points back to the Son's preexistent enthroning alongside the Father, where they shared "with" each other in all things (see chap. 1).

Jesus goes a step further in an argument with his opponents about whether he is indeed the Messiah/*christos* (John 10:24). In classic fashion, Jesus takes things in a direction they probably did not expect. He affirms, somewhat indirectly, that his mighty deeds prove that he is indeed the Messiah. But then he stretches their category for "Son of God" (10:36) by saying, "I and the Father are one" (10:30), and "The Father is in me, and I am in the Father" (10:38). No mere human king could make such a striking claim: to be fully one with God, as Son and Father mysteriously "in" each other. He repeats this claim later, when, directly addressing God this time, he says, "You, Father, are in me, and I in you. . . . We are one" (17:21–22). Finally, recall how, when Jesus speaks of his own preexistence moments earlier (17:5), he addresses his "Father" and asks, "Glorify me . . . with the glory that I had with you," reiterating the intimacy of their relation even from before creation.

As with various examples mentioned in chapter 1 of this book, many New Testament scholars pump the brakes at this point and claim that these statements were fabricated and later placed on the lips of Jesus. But without wading too far into such waters, I would offer up a key passage demonstrating the reasonableness in thinking that the ideas expressed in John 8; 10; and 17 reflect what Jesus actually taught. In both Matthew (11:25–27) and Luke (10:21–22), Jesus makes a statement that is widely accepted as authentic by even the most critical of scholars.[7] This saying is often called the "Johannine thunderbolt," because it seems like it would fit in the Gospel of John but instead breaks forth in two of the Synoptic Gospels. It is worth quoting in full:

> In that same hour he rejoiced in the Holy Spirit and said, "I thank you, Father, Lord of heaven and earth, that you have hidden these things from the wise and understanding and revealed them to little children; yes, Father, for such was your gracious will. All things have been handed over to me by my Father, and no one knows who the Son is except

---

7. It has long been considered (by scholars who hold to a particular view of the origins of the Synoptic Gospels) to have been part of the pre-Gospel source "Q."

the Father, or who the Father is except the Son and anyone
to whom the Son chooses to reveal him." (Luke 10:21–22)

Observe the intense Father-Son language. Jesus thanks the Father for revealing himself to the Son, such that no one can understand the Father except through the Son. It is a striking claim.
Infinitely more than even the most devoted marriage or friend-
ship, the essence of their relationship as Father and Son is one
of mutual *knowing*, or mutual *revealing*. The Father knows the
Son in an exclusive way, and the Son knows the Father in an
exclusive way. No other figure, royal or otherwise, can approach
the uniqueness of this divine relationship. That is who they are
as Father and Son. That is the definition of their existence. That
is what it means to be the triune God. The persons exhaustively
know and reveal one another. The Johannine thunderbolt is one
of the highest expressions of divine Christology found in the
early Jesus traditions behind the Synoptic Gospels.

And the fact that John 10:15 records the same thing ("The
Father knows me and I know the Father") is strong evidence
that such stunning statements in John's Gospel are not imagina-
tive fabrications but go back to the very words of Jesus himself.[8]

What, then, does "Son of God" mean according to these
examples? It means that the Father and his Son share a divine
relationship unlike any other.

An Eternally Begotten Son

I began this chapter by introducing how "Son of God" can be
used in essentially two ways. First, similar to how such language worked in the ancient world and the Old Testament,

---

8. For further development of this idea, see Mark Goodacre, "Johannine Thunderbolt or Synoptic Seed? Matt. 11:27 // Luke 10:22 in Christological Context" (paper
presented at the Annual Meeting of the Society of Biblical Literature, San Antonio, TX,
November 2016).

"Son of God" *can* simply denote a king or messiah, and it is applied to Jesus in this way at points in the New Testament. But second, I have attempted to demonstrate that this "Son of God" language can go beyond messiahship. It is also used in the New Testament to show how the Son shares fully in what makes the Father truly God. It is a way of expressing an eternal relation they share even before Jesus's fleshly birth. A few other passages help us put this all together.

As surveyed in chapter 1, four verses that deal with how Jesus has "come" or was "sent" into the world also feature "Son" language (John 3:17; Rom. 8:3; Gal. 4:4; 1 John 4:9). To this we can add the more precise phrasing "Son of God" reflected in 1 John 5:20, where the apostle writes, "We know that the Son of God has come." Note the sequencing: this person *already was* the "Son of God," and then he came (in the flesh). He did not become the "Son of God" when he was designated a messianic king, but he already was the "Son of God" before he even came. Put differently, this passage, alongside the other four, makes clear that "Son of God" is not merely a messianic label but points to the divine essence of this "Son," since "Son" is essential to his identity long before his earthly coming.

Paul elsewhere reflects this same logic. In Romans 1:3b–4, Paul describes the two main aspects of Jesus's ministry: his messianic mission as the royal heir "from David according to the flesh" and his exaltation as "Son of God in power . . . by his resurrection from the dead." On the surface it seems that this second clause, where "Son of God" is used, indicates that Jesus was transformed into or adopted as such upon his resurrection—and that he was not "Son of God" before then. But this would be a misreading.[9] Paul carefully states that Jesus is

---

9. A fuller examination of this kind of "adoptionist" Christology is provided by Michael F. Bird, *Jesus the Eternal Son: Answering Adoptionist Christology* (Grand Rapids, MI: Eerdmans, 2017).

"declared" (Gk. *horisthentos*) to be the "Son of God in power." The "declared" and "in power" are key: the resurrection and ascension of Jesus do not turn him into the "Son of God" (as if he were not the "Son of God" beforehand) but signal his *power* over all the universe after accomplishing salvation. Importantly, this twofold movement of humiliation-exaltation in Romans 1:3b–4 is building on a key statement in 1:3a. Paul writes that God prepromised the gospel in the holy Scriptures and that this gospel was "concerning his Son." He *already was*—and always was—the divine "Son" before his earthly ministry (1:3a), and *then* he was enfleshed as a Davidic Messiah, put to death, resurrected, and (re)seated in full power (1:3b–4).

Let one final piece of evidence be marshaled. The apostle John famously declares Jesus to be the *monogenēs* of God five times. There remains much debate about whether *monogenēs* is best understood as "only" or "only begotten" (thus, English translations vary).[10] Let us look at the way each is stated to shed some light on the matter (all my trans.):

- John 1:14: "glory as *monogenous* of the Father"
- John 1:18: "*monogenēs* . . . who is at the side of the Father"
- John 3:16: "he gave his *monogenē* Son"
- John 3:18: "the name of the *monogenous* Son of God"
- 1 John 4:9: "God sent his *monogenē* Son into the world"

In the latter three instances, the word "Son" is explicitly used, while "Father" appears in the first two. So across all five verses, Father-Son language is already present. Thus, *monogenēs*

---

10. Common translations of *monogenēs* include "only begotten" (KJV, NKJV), "one and only" (CSB, NET, NIV), "only" (ESV, RSV), "unique" or "one of a kind" (NASB footnote). The most thorough recent analysis of this word is Charles Lee Irons, "A Lexical Defense of the Johannine 'Only Begotten,'" in *Retrieving Eternal Generation*, ed. Fred Sanders and Scott R. Swain (Grand Rapids, MI: Zondervan, 2017), 98–116.

adds something new to the mix. It is making a stronger statement than "Son" can make by itself. Jesus Christ is *distinctly*, *uniquely* the "Son" of the Father. From before all time, he and he alone is defined, as to the core of his very being, to be the truly unparalleled Son of the Father.

So whether the word *monogenēs* by itself should be translated "only begotten" is not really the point. The term marks the second person of the Trinity off as uniquely the one who is from the Father—who distinctly shares unity with him. His existence is and always has been one of eternal "Son" in relation to the eternal "Father." And that is the essence of divine "begetting" in the first place.

Summary

In this chapter I have aimed to show how "son of God" (as a royal label) underwent a powerful transformation to "Son of God" (as an indication of divinity) in the hands of the New Testament authors. What led them to this conclusion?

Certainly, the apostolic encounter with the actual person and teachings of Jesus was the decisive factor for their leaping this gap. But one might also look to the Old Testament as a source that gently nudged them in this direction. Perhaps the most impressive potential influence is Isaiah 9:6–7. Though this text is not cited directly in the New Testament, the influence of Isaiah on the New Testament authors ranks second only to that of the Psalms. Isaiah 9 is the capstone of a sequence of promises concerning symbolic sons, who will be given names evoking God's judgment and restoration: "Shear-Jashub" (i.e., "A remnant will return," 7:3), "Immanuel" (i.e., "God with us," 7:14), and "Maher-shalal-hash-baz" (i.e., "Quick to the plunder, swift to the spoils," 8:1–3). A climax is reached when Isaiah foretells the coming of a "son" who will sit on David's throne forever

(9:6–7). So far, so good: this fits with conventional ancient use of "son" for a king.

But then Isaiah reveals the names of this symbolic son: "Wonderful Counselor, Mighty God, Everlasting Father, Prince of Peace" (9:6). These stunning names, particularly "God" and "Father," suggest that, in Isaiah's mind, there is something about this future "son" that stretches all human boundaries. (Unsurprisingly, early Greek and Aramaic translators of this passage struggled with how to take these names.)[11] Isaiah leaves the tension tantalizingly unresolved: "the LORD" remains distinct from this Davidic king (9:7), yet this future enthroned "son" is called "God" (9:6). Perhaps Isaiah's striking prediction provides the New Testament authors and Jesus himself with the categories by which they, in the fullness of time, could articulate Jesus's own identity as *divine* "Son" in the same way.

Pulling all these threads together, then, provides strong confirmation that the church fathers were not innovating when they developed the creeds. Though some of the particular phrasing may have been formalized later, the New Testament authors—following Jesus himself and, perhaps, Isaiah—had already arrived at that conclusion.

Not only is Jesus the "Son of God" as a messianic king, but he is more than that. He is, and always has been, "God the Son" as well.

So What?

It is worth reflecting on how Jesus's use of Abba—and the full depth of his sonship to the Father—might shape how Christians should think of their own relationship to the Father. We

---

11. The main tradition of Greek Isaiah renders the name "Angel of Great Counsel"; Targum Pseudo-Jonathan renders it "Wonderful Counselor, Mighty God enduring forever, the Messiah."

are urged by the Spirit to, like Jesus, call out to "Abba" in Romans 8:15 and Galatians 4:6. By virtue of the eternal sonship of Jesus Christ, our relationship to the living God has been transformed from one of enemy to one of adopted sons and daughters.

3

Christ the *Kyrios*

Reading the Old Testament Afresh

In late eighteenth-century England, Josiah Wedgwood was a household name. He was an entrepreneur in domestic pottery, vases, and other home goods, and his pioneering work in mass-marketing to sell those products largely fueled the consumer revolution of the period.

He was also a staunch abolitionist devoted to the cause of eliminating the scourge of slavery from Britain. And in 1787 he came upon a way to reach the masses with the message. He designed what became known as the "Wedgwood medallion," which was emblazoned with the picture of a slave in shackles and the statement "Am I not a man and a brother?" In one deft stroke, the medallion simultaneously appealed to post-Enlightenment humanism (dignity of man and brotherhood of mankind) *and* the fashion sensibilities of the upper and middle classes. Soon high-society women were wearing the medallion as part of bracelets, brooches, and hairpins. In short, to undermine the slave trade, Wedgwood appealed directly to the moral and fashion tastes of the very classes that had so long depended on slavery for their standard of living. The medallion used the very things that were important to society's elites to convince them to change their views.

This kind of move—making a case for something by using the raw materials provided by the very people you are trying to convince—is at once subtle and extremely powerful. And when one turns to the early Christian confession of the full divine essence of Jesus Christ, this very same move is on full display.

Central to the Old Testament and all Jewish thought is the affirmation that there is one God. This strong form of "monotheism" is the calling card of biblical religion, particularly in an ancient world that was full of many "so-called gods" (1 Cor. 8:5). It is worth asking, then, How do the earliest Christians, most of whom grew up Jewish and were heirs to this strong monotheistic heritage, express their renewed understanding of it? Specifically, how do they affirm monotheism *and* proclaim Jesus Christ as fully God *without* suggesting that they believe in two or more gods? Surprisingly, and quite powerfully, they use the Old Testament to do it. To make the case that Jesus Christ is truly God, they use the very source text that asserts monotheism in the first place.

This chapter surveys how the New Testament authors, through interacting with Scripture in profound ways, make clear that the one true God revealed in the Old Testament is now fully disclosed to include (and to have always included) the divine Son. It is essential that the New Testament authors employ the Old Testament to prove Jesus's divinity because if he is truly God, he must be the "God of the Old Testament" and not just the "God of the New Testament."

Calling Jesus "Lord"

In any culture, what you call someone says a lot about him or her. And when it comes to what Scripture calls Jesus, it is worth slowing down and examining it closely.

The most common words used to refer to God in the Hebrew Old Testament are "Lord" (*Adonai*), "God" (*El* or *Elohim*), and "LORD" (YHWH). The latter is the most frequent (nearly 7,000x) and also the most fascinating. It is still uncertain exactly how YHWH was pronounced in ancient Israel, and eventually within Judaism it was deemed unspeakable; rather, *Adonai* was typically read in its place.[1]

Representing YHWH in writing has also been tricky. Some Jews in the Dead Sea area in the 200s–100s BC left a gap in the Hebrew text where YHWH belonged and then inked it with archaic letters,[2] while others wrote * * * * instead of the letters themselves.[3] As Jews began translating the Hebrew Old Testament into Greek at an early stage, some retained YHWH with Hebrew letters.[4] Some used the Greek letters *IAŌ*, as a rough approximation of the pronunciation.[5] And some mimicked the appearance of the Hebrew letters (יהוה) with the approximate Greek equivalents (ΠΙΠΙ), that is, *PIPI*.[6]

But instead of retaining a Hebrew-like word, some Jewish translators began making a substitution for YHWH: using the Greek Lord/*kyrios* as a replacement for what they spoke aloud (*Adonai*).[7] By the first century AD, it appears that this practice

---

1. The modern debate about whether to pronounce the divine name YHWH as "Yahweh" or "Jehovah" largely stems from questions about which vowels to use between the letters ("a . . . e" or "e . . . o . . . a").
2. E.g., 4Q161; 11Q5.
3. E.g., 4Q175.
4. E.g., 8HevXII; papyrus Fouad 266.
5. E.g., 4Q120 of Lev. 4.
6. This is even noted by Jerome in his AD 384 epistle to Marcella.
7. Josephus, a first-century Greek Jew, comments, "*Adonai* in Hebrew speech means *kyrios*." *Ant.* 5.121.

was spreading among Greek-speaking Jews,[8] for whom the use of a Greek equivalent made more sense than the use of a word in a language (Hebrew) they could no longer speak or read. We do the same in English today with "LORD."

Why does all this matter? Simply this: early Christians applied the same word Lord/*kyrios* to Jesus Christ immediately in the early church. Across nearly every New Testament writing and throughout early Christian sources, Jesus is called Lord/*kyrios*. And according to the Gospel writers, he is called *kyrios* even during his earthly ministry (e.g., Mark 11:3), not just afterward. Yes, sometimes the use of Lord/*kyrios* (particularly in the vocative) can simply be a sign of respect, but by no means do all the hundreds of occurrences in the New Testament fall into that category. Thus, the evidence is clear that early Christians immediately, and apparently with no qualms, took what had become a default Greek word used for YHWH (and *Adonai*) and applied it directly to Jesus Christ.

This practice leads to some fuzziness in the way the New Testament uses Lord/*kyrios*: Does the term refer to God the Father or God the Son? Luke 1–2 provides a capital example.[9] The word appears about twenty-seven times in these two chapters. The Father is clearly meant in twenty-three of them. But in two cases, the unborn (1:43) or recently born (2:11) Jesus is called Lord/*kyrios*. This side-by-side use of Lord/*kyrios* for both God the Father and the baby Jesus is simply stunning. But there are also two examples that leave us a bit in the air: John the Baptist will fulfill Old Testament prophecies by going before the Lord/*kyrios* (1:17, 76), but to whom is that referring? This fuzzy use of Lord/*kyrios* seems intentional: Luke

---

8. E.g., Philo, *Leg.* 1.48 (using *kyrios* when quoting an Old Testament passage that reads YHWH) and other places; Josephus, *Ant.* 13.68–69.

9. For further discussion, see C. Kavin Rowe, *Early Narrative Christology: The Lord in the Gospel of Luke*, BZNW 139 (Berlin: de Gruyter, 2006).

is suggesting that both Father and Son are the same "Lord," though distinct in personhood.

Other signs of this usage are found in the New Testament. For instance, New Testament authors occasionally refer to the "word of the Lord/*kyrios*" (Acts 13:48–49; 1 Thess. 4:15) but do not specify whether they are referring to the common Old Testament formula used for God's word or a word directly from Jesus—or both. Likewise, the "day of the Lord/*kyrios*"— a prominent Old Testament motif referring to God's return in judgment—is at times applied to Jesus directly (1 Cor. 1:8; 2 Cor. 1:14) but is fuzzy in other places (1 Cor. 5:5; 1 Thess. 5:2).

This use of Lord/*kyrios* to refer to Jesus is perhaps most pronounced in what appear to be early Christian creedal statements. Central to the faith of the people of God is the confession that the true God is YHWH or Lord/*kyrios*—not Moloch, Ba'al, Dagon, Ra, Zeus, or anyone else. It is fascinating, then, that early Christians made not only confessing Jesus to be "Savior" a central part of their faith but also confessing him to be Lord/*kyrios*. In four passages that may give insight into early church creeds (Acts 10:36; Rom. 10:9; 1 Cor. 12:3; Phil. 2:11), the declaration "Jesus is Lord/*kyrios*" appears to function as a kind of line in the sand for early orthodoxy.

Though it is easy for Christians today to use "Lord" for Jesus without a second thought, it was a far more consequential statement in the early church. The early, widespread, and flexible use of Lord/*kyrios*—as derived from YHWH—for both Father and Son suggests that Jesus's followers believed them to be mutually the same God.

Applying YHWH Passages to Jesus

Given that early Christians unanimously called Jesus the Lord/ *kyrios* they knew from the Old Testament, another fascinating pattern becomes easier to understand: taking passages from the Old Testament that refer explicitly to YHWH and applying them to Jesus. Let us examine a few of these.[10]

Mark begins his Gospel with a fascinating statement: the "gospel of Jesus Christ" is that which was "written in Isaiah the prophet" (Mark 1:1–2). Then he links together Old Testament quotations to show *where* this gospel of Jesus was written. Mark's first phrase ("Behold, I send my messenger before your face, who will prepare your way," Mark 1:2) is from Malachi 3:1 (and perhaps Ex. 23:20). Mark's second phrase ("The voice of the one crying in the wilderness: 'Prepare the way of the Lord, make his paths straight,'" Mark 1:3) is from Isaiah 40:3. So far so good.

But we should, as always, look up those passages in the Old Testament to find out what Mark is doing with them. And when we do, a striking thing surfaces. In Malachi 3:1, the speaker is YHWH, and he is sending the messenger to go before and "prepare the way *before me*." And the same is true in Isaiah 40:3: the voice is to "prepare the way of *the* Lord [i.e., YHWH]" and "make straight . . . a highway for *our God*." Only a few verses later, the herald is exhorted to call out, "Behold your God!" (Isa. 40:9). Note what is going on in both Malachi and Isaiah: the messenger precedes *YHWH himself*.

Mark, then, is bringing out a fuller significance. He quotes these Old Testament passages as being spoken by God, who is the "I" sending the messenger that is fulfilled in John the Baptist (coming on the scene in Mark 1:4). But Mark makes a tweak to both Malachi and Isaiah: the "way" and the "paths" that in the Old Testament belong to YHWH himself now be-

---

10. For details on such uses of the Old Testament in the New, see especially David B. Capes, *The Divine Christ: Paul, the Lord Jesus, and the Scriptures of Israel* (Grand Rapids, MI: Baker Academic, 2018); Gordon Fee, *Pauline Christology: An Exegetical-Theological Study* (Peabody, MA: Hendrickson, 2007).

long to "you." And who is that "you"? Jesus himself, who appears immediately after John the Baptist. In other words, Mark has taken two important passages in the Old Testament that describe how a future messenger will prepare the way for YHWH (not for a human messiah, as often misunderstood) and has now shown that he is preparing the way for Jesus *as the incarnate God himself.*[11]

Let us consider another example. In Acts 2, Peter delivers his famous Pentecost sermon. Near the end of the sermon, Peter exhorts all to call on and be baptized "in the name of Jesus Christ" (2:38). Why? Because "everyone who calls upon the name of the Lord shall be saved" (2:21). Simple enough—until you realize that he is quoting from the Old Testament. And if you look up the passage he is quoting (Joel 2:28–32), you find that Joel says, "Everyone who calls on the name of YHWH will be saved" (my trans.). See what has happened? In Joel, we are to call on the name of YHWH. Interpreted by Peter, this is now understood to be the Lord/*kyrios*, Jesus Christ. And Paul treats this Joel passage the same way in Romans 10:13. In explaining why the confession "Jesus is Lord/*kyrios*" brings salvation (Rom. 10:9, recall above), he likewise equates the "name of YHWH" from Joel with the name of Jesus Christ.[12]

The book of Revelation features a sophisticated way in which Old Testament designations for YHWH are, in effect, shared by Father and Son. The recurring phrase "first and last" (and the derived form "Alpha and Omega") is directly from Isaiah 41:4; 44:6; and 48:12—each of which emphatically declares

---

11. Furthermore, Mark 1:1 also features a very famous textual variant. At the end of the verse, some manuscripts read, "the Son of God," while others do not. Recent research suggests that it was likely original. See Tommy Wasserman, "The 'Son of God' Was in the Beginning (Mark 1:1)," *JTS* 62, no. 1 (2011): 20–50. Either way, Mark's explosive introduction to his Gospel makes clear that he does believe Jesus to be the divine "Son" in the fullest possible way.

12. See the insightful study by C. Kavin Rowe, "Romans 10:13: What Is the Name of the Lord?," *HBT* 22, no. 1 (2000): 135–73.

the uniqueness of YHWH as the one true God. But in Revelation, an interesting thing happens: this phrase is applied to God the Father in 1:8, to the Son in 1:17 and 22:13, and (apparently) to both in 21:6.[13]

Other instances could be mentioned. When Jesus inspects the temple and declares it a "den of robbers" (Luke 19:45–46), he is quoting what YHWH says about his own inspection of the temple in Jeremiah 7:11–15. Paul quotes Jeremiah 9:23 ("Let him who boasts boast . . . that I am the LORD") but applies it to Christ in 1 Corinthians 1:31. And in 1 Corinthians 2:16, the "mind of the Lord" (Isa. 40:13, in Gk. translation) becomes the "mind of Christ." In each example, the New Testament applies a YHWH passage from the Old Testament to Christ without batting an eyelash.

But arguably the most impressive example of this kind of refreshed reading of the Old Testament is found in 1 Corinthians 8.[14] In 8:1–5, Paul instructs the Corinthian church about meat sacrificed to pagan gods. To dispute the existence of such fake gods, he weaves together the wording ("carved image" / "idol," "gods," "heaven," "earth") of the first and second commandments in Deuteronomy 5:7–8. Then he says the following in 1 Corinthians 8:6: "For us there is one God, the Father, . . . and one Lord, Jesus Christ." This phrasing is drawn from the key monotheistic verse in the very next chapter of Deuteronomy, the Shema: "The LORD our God, the LORD is one" (Deut. 6:4, where "LORD" in English represents YHWH).

There are four building blocks in this classic confession: "our," "God," "LORD," and "one." And all four are rearranged

---

13. It is declared by a "voice from the throne" (Rev. 21:3), which at this stage in Revelation is shared by Father and Son.

14. See the detailed analysis in Erik Waaler, *The Shema and the First Commandment in First Corinthians: An Intertextual Approach to Paul's Re-Reading of Deuteronomy*, WUNT, 2nd ser., vol. 253 (Tübingen: Mohr Siebeck, 2008).

in Paul's statement: "us . . . one . . . God . . . one . . . Lord."
In light of the practice discussed earlier, where the Greek word
used to translate YHWH is applied to Jesus Christ regularly in
the New Testament, it is possible to trace precisely what Paul
has done:

Deuteronomy 6:4		1 Corinthians 8:6
"our God"	→	"For us . . . one God, the Father"
"the LORD is one"	→	"one Lord/*kyrios*, Jesus Christ"

Paul is laboring to make a core Christian belief clear. We are
still monotheists who confess the Shema. But with the coming
of Christ, the veil has been pulled back so that the nature of
this monotheism is understood more robustly: the one "LORD/
God" of the Shema is now fully revealed to be (and always to
have been) Father and Son. By carefully mapping "God" to
Father and "Lord" to Son in this verse—but elsewhere doing
the opposite, mapping "Lord" to Father (regularly) and "God"
to Son (see chap. 6, below)—Paul is affirming that "God" and
"Lord" refer to *both* "Father" and "Son" in equal measure.
For they are one.

Let us step back to gaze on the mastery of this move. To
make his point about the full divinity of Jesus Christ—in a discussion about the very risk of pagan polytheism—Paul goes to
the heart of Israelite monotheism itself. He reveals that the Shema's claims about our "one" true "God" should be understood
to include the Son, who is just as much "Lord" as the Father. A
higher claim on behalf of Christ could hardly be conceived of.
Paul's "splitting" of the Shema (as some describe it) is one of
the best examples of his divine Christology.

In all likelihood, Paul is simply taking a page from Jesus's own
playbook. Recall that twice in the Gospel of John, Jesus claims

to be "one" with "the Father" (10:30; 17:22). This claim is probably an allusion to the Shema: the decisive attribute of *oneness* at the heart of Israel's faith is applied to Father and Son together. They are fully one yet distinguished. And the striking thing is that the Old Testament is used to prove this.

Like Father, Like Son

So far I have covered evidence showing that Jesus receives the Old Testament name of the Godhead (YHWH/*kyrios*) and that the earliest Christians interpreted various Old Testament passages speaking of YHWH as mysteriously including the Son—all while maintaining monotheism. But we can carry this strategy one step further.

There are certain things that only God *is* or *does*, which no one else—not even an exalted angel—can share in. This reality puts a chasm between God and his creatures. And by two different patterns in the New Testament, Jesus Christ is clearly on God's side of that chasm, where he *is* or *does* that which characterizes only God. In this way he is fully identified not just *with* but *as* the God of Israel.

Divine Prerogatives

The first pattern found in the New Testament is ascribing certain exclusive prerogatives of God to Jesus.[15] By "exclusive prerogative," I mean a role that belongs only to a certain person, which cannot be fully delegated to someone else. Let me illustrate. The president of the United States bears many responsibilities that, in practice, are actually executed

---

15. The most influential study on this pattern for Paul is Richard J. Bauckham, *Jesus and the God of Israel: God Crucified and Other Studies on the New Testament's Christology of Divine Identity* (Grand Rapids, MI: Eerdmans, 2008). Richard Hays has applied Bauckham's insights to the Gospels in *Echoes of Scripture in the Gospels* (Waco, TX: Baylor University Press, 2016).

by someone else. For instance, though the president is commander in chief of the armed forces, this role is actually carried out day to day by a variety of subordinate generals. Some prerogatives, however, such as legislative veto power, belong to the president and the president only, and they can never be delegated.

On a much grander scale, many of God's actions are carried out day to day by angels, prophets, and so on. They represent him and do his bidding; their authority is delegated to them by God. But God also holds some exclusive prerogatives that cannot be shared.

The most decisive are creation of and sovereignty over "all things," with a strong emphasis on "all." A central tenet of the Old Testament, as well as subsequent Jewish literature, is that God and God alone directly created "all things" and bears absolute authority over "all things." In fact, divine creation of "all things" is the starting point of all biblical revelation (Gen. 1), and no one is ever seen to compete with God for this role in Scripture.[16]

Likewise, while heavenly or earthly subordinates may have a role in managing aspects of creation as designated by God, he and he alone is described as reigning and ruling over "all things," that is, over the entire universe. One might even say that these two exclusive prerogatives are the ultimate litmus test for what it means to be God. And though it may have shocked Jewish ears, precisely these two exclusive prerogatives are ascribed to Jesus early and uniformly in the New Testament.

---

16. The Old Testament occasionally describes "wisdom" as present at and instrumental in creation (Prov. 8:22–23), but this is best understood not as a quasi-being distinct from God but as a personified attribute of God. On this point, see Larry Hurtado, *One God, One Lord: Early Christian Devotion and Ancient Jewish Monotheism* (London: SCM, 1988), 37–48. For a broader critique of so-called "wisdom Christology," see Grant Macaskill, *Revealed Wisdom and Inaugurated Eschatology in Ancient Judaism and Early Christianity*, JSJSup 115 (Leiden: Brill, 2007).

In terms of creation, the New Testament makes it clear that the preexistent Son of God is also the Creator of all things. Five passages describe the creation of "all things" (Gk. *ta panta*) or "the world" (Gk. *kosmos*) using nearly identical language. But through a subtle use of prepositions, they attribute this act of creation to both Father and Son:

Creation is . . .	"from/by" (Gk. *ek/en*)	"through" (Gk. *dia*)	"unto" (Gk. *eis*)
John 1:3	–	Son	–
Rom. 11:36	God/Father	God/Father	God/Father
1 Cor. 8:6	God/Father	Son	God/Father
Col. 1:16	Son	Son	Son
Heb. 1:2	–	Son	–

Applying these three aspects of the creation of "all things" to the Father is rather normal—but applying them to the Son is earth-shattering. He is not just an "instrument" of creation (whatever that would mean) but is as fully the Creator as the Father. They are not divided but united as one God who created "all things."[17]

The same is true for sovereignty over "all things." Jesus claims that "*all* authority in heaven and on earth" has been given to him (Matt. 28:18). Paul writes that "*all* things" (3x) are in subjection to Christ (1 Cor. 15:27), that he is enthroned "far above *all* rule and authority and power and dominion" both now and in the future (Eph. 1:21), and that he is the head of "*all* rule and authority" (Col. 2:10). The repeated use of "all" drives home the fact that the all-encompassing authority of Jesus is not limited in any way. This can only ever be said about the true God

---

17. See this book's conclusion for additional discussion about the nature of this creative act according to John 1:1–3.

of Israel.[18] For good reason, John sees "the Lamb" seated on the same (singular) heavenly throne as God the Father, where they rule over all things together as one (Rev. 7:17).

A handful of other divine prerogatives follow closely behind creation of and sovereignty over "all things." Jesus Christ claims to forgive sins between other parties (not just sins committed against himself), which immediately causes his Jewish opponents to balk: "Who can forgive sins but God alone?" (Mark 2:7). Christ exercises a stunning ability to control nature and the weather (Luke 8:24–25), which God alone does in the Old Testament (Ps. 107:25). Jesus is able to penetrate the secret thoughts of people he meets (e.g., Luke 5:17–26; 6:6–11), which is an ability God alone possesses (Matt. 6:18).[19] He enacts the "visitation" of judgment and salvation (Luke 1:78; 7:16; 19:44), which, in the Old Testament and in Jewish writings, is always understood to be a "visitation" of God himself.[20] Christ will execute final punishment on the wicked with "the breath of his mouth" (2 Thess. 2:8), which is a prerogative of God in the Old Testament (Isa. 11:4).

Against such a background, a deft juxtaposition by Luke can be seen in a clearer light: the casting out of demons is

---

18. Some scholars point to the enthroning of the "Son of Man" in 1 En. 61–62 and of Moses in Ezek. Trag. 66–89 as exceptions to this rule; however, their reigns appear to be of a delegated sort and are purely in visions/dreams, not reality. See the discussion in Richard Bauckham, "The Throne of God and the Worship of Jesus," in *The Jewish Roots of Christological Monotheism: Papers from the St. Andrews Conference on the Historical Origins of the Worship of Jesus*, ed. Cary C. Newman, James R. Davila, and Gladys S. Lewis, JSJSup 63 (Leiden: Brill, 1999), 43–69.

19. This theme is traced out in detail in Collin Bullard, *Jesus and the Thoughts of Many Hearts: Implicit Christology and Jesus' Knowledge in the Gospel of Luke*, LNTS 530 (London: T&T Clark, 2015).

20. This "visitation" theme is found in several texts, including Gen. 50:24; Isa. 10:3; Jer. 29:10–14; Sir. 35:18; Pss. Sol. 11.1–6; 4 Ezra 6.18–19; 1QS 4:18–19. For a detailed discussion, see Gregory R. Lanier, "Luke's Distinctive Use of the Temple: Portraying the Divine Visitation," *JTS* 65, no. 2 (2014): 433–62. The related "coming of God" theme is examined by Edward Adams, "The Coming of God Tradition and Its Influence on New Testament Parousia Texts," in *Biblical Traditions in Transmission: Essays in Honour of Michael A. Knibb*, ed. Charlotte Hempel and Judith M. Lieu, JSJSup 111 (Leiden: Brill, 2006), 1–19.

simultaneously acclaimed as "how much God has done" and "how much Jesus [has] done" (Luke 8:39).[21]

These prerogatives are not "messianic" per se. Little in the Old Testament or Judaism anticipates that a messiah figure would perform these divine acts. Rather, they *become* messianic in the New Testament because of who does them: Jesus Christ.

Divine Metaphors

A second and less well-known pattern in the New Testament is that of taking divine metaphors and remapping them to Jesus. In recent decades, the study of metaphors in the Old and New Testaments has taken on new life. Metaphors are ways we conceive of something abstract in terms of things we know. For instance, one may think of marriage as a "journey" (with travelers, a destination, and so forth). Or one may think of a career as a "battle" (winning a promotion) or a "ladder" (climbing higher than your peers). Metaphors are not just clever things we do with words, but they both shape and reflect how we think about the world.

And Scripture is full of them, particularly when it comes to understanding and relating to God himself. What sets Israelite religion apart from that of its peers is how YHWH takes no physical or visible form. He is pure spirit. But one way the biblical authors express their relationship with an immaterial God is through metaphors—that is, describing his abstract characteristics through concrete things we know. For example, the Old Testament describes God metaphorically as a warrior (Jer. 20:11), fortress (2 Sam. 22:2), bear (Hos. 13:8), refiner (Mal. 3:3), knitter (Ps. 139:13), lion (Job 10:16), fire (Deut. 4:24), and so on. He is not *literally* any one of these, for he is pure God. But

---

21. Moreover, these demons are afraid that Jesus has come to cast them "into the abyss" (Luke 8:31), which is an eschatological prerogative only God possesses.

his people relate to him in deep, fundamental ways by using these complex metaphors to describe him. We *think* of him as a shelter (Ps. 91:1), as a shield (Ps. 18:2), as a potter with clay (Isa. 64:8).

In a few fascinating instances, such deeply embedded metaphors for God are taken up in the New Testament and applied to Jesus Christ. A few may be listed.[22] In Isaiah 8:14 God himself is a "stone" and "rock" that can either protect or crush his people; at the end of the parable of the tenants (Matt. 21:44; Luke 20:18), this "stone" metaphor is reconfigured such that Christ is that "crushing" stone.[23] God alone is described as the "horn of my salvation" (2 Sam. 22:3; Ps. 18:2), but this metaphor of power and deliverance is applied to Jesus (Luke 1:69). At various points in the Old Testament, God is understood metaphorically not just as "light" but more specifically as the "dawn" of the sun, bringing deliverance to his people (Deut. 33:2; Isa. 58:8; Hos. 6:3; Mal. 4:2); in the New Testament, this vivid metaphor is attributed to Jesus (Luke 1:78). God alone is portrayed as "mother bird" of the Israelites in the Old Testament (Ex. 19:4; Deut. 32:11–12; Ps. 17:8), but Jesus takes this metaphor on himself (Matt. 23:37; Luke 13:34).[24] Throughout the Old Testament, God reveals himself to be the "bridegroom" or "husband" of his people (especially in Hosea, Jeremiah, Ezekiel, and Ps. 45), but this metaphor is applied to

---

22. For additional detail, consult Gregory R. Lanier, *Old Testament Conceptual Metaphors and the Christology of Luke's Gospel*, LNTS 591 (London: T&T Clark, 2018); Sigurd Grindheim, *God's Equal: What Can We Know about Jesus' Self-Understanding in the Synoptic Gospels*, LNTS 446 (London: T&T Clark, 2011), esp. chap. 7. Additionally, some of the Lukan metaphors are discussed in Nina Henrichs-Tarasenkova, *Luke's Christology of Divine Identity*, LNTS 224 (London: T&T Clark, 2015), chap. 5, while the "bridegroom" metaphor is analyzed in detail in Michael Tait, *Jesus, the Divine Bridegroom, in Mark 2:18–22: Mark's Christology Upgraded*, AnBib 185 (Roma: Gregorian and Biblical Press, 2010).

23. Paul's use of the same stone passages also alludes to Jesus's divine identity. He first introduces the Isaiah stone in Rom. 9:33, where "whoever believes in him" in Isa. 28:16 most likely refers to God. In Rom. 10:11, he repeats part of the quotation but has redirected it to Jesus as the one in whom we should believe.

24. See Jonathan Rowlands, "Jesus and the Wings of YHWH: Bird Imagery in the Lament over Jerusalem (Matt 23:37–39; Luke 13:34–35)," *NovT* 61, no. 2 (2019): 115–36.

Jesus several times (Mark 2:19–20; John 3:29; Rev. 21:2). Finally, God reveals himself as the chief "shepherd" who rescues his lost sheep (Ezek. 34:1–16), and then Jesus expresses his own identity the same way (John 10:1–18).

The identity of Jesus is, no doubt, expressed through other Old Testament metaphors that are not divine, such as "root of Jesse" (Isa. 11:10; cf. Rev. 22:16) or lion of Judah (Gen. 49:10; Rev. 5:5). But the *divine conceptual metaphors* listed here are a rich means by which the authors of the Old Testament articulate something essential about God. And in the hands of the New Testament authors, they are remapped to Jesus Christ. That is, when the New Testament authors think about God as stone/ rock, horn, dawn, mother bird, bridegroom, or shepherd—*they think of Jesus*.

In sum, the New Testament employs two patterns—divine prerogatives and divine metaphors—to demonstrate a key truth: like Father, like Son. That which is exclusive to the Father in the Old Testament is fully revealed in the New Testament to incorporate the Son in a powerful way. Jesus is and does that which no angel or prophet or mere human messiah has the right or ability to do: namely, the very things that make the Father to be God.

Egō Eimi ("I Am")

The burden of this chapter has been to show how the New Testament authors read the Scriptures of Israel afresh to demonstrate not only that Jesus Christ is "a man attested to you by God" (Acts 2:22) but that he is fully God. The striking thing is that they use the Old Testament itself to prove this point. Where did they come up with such an idea?

It is possible that they were simply bringing out what was already there in texts like Isaiah 9:6 or Daniel 7:14, which we discussed previously. But it is likely that they were also taking their cue from Jesus himself, particularly his famous use of the catchphrase "I am."

This phrase takes one of two forms. The first is "I am ____," where the blank is filled with a predicate, like "the bread of life" (John 6:35), "the light of the world" (8:12), "the door" (10:7), "the vine" (15:1), and so forth. These miniature parables are significant descriptions of the richness of who Jesus is.

But the second, and perhaps more intriguing, form of the phrase is "I am" (Gk. *egō eimi*) by itself, with no predicate. In Greek (or any language), there is nothing magical about this phrase. But in various situations in the New Testament, Jesus speaks these two words in a way that suggests that more is going on. As he exercises the divine prerogative of calming the storm, he declares, "Take heart, *egō eimi*," which immediately causes the disciples to be "utterly astounded" (Mark 6:50–51, my trans.). After walking on water, Jesus tells his disciples, "*Egō eimi*; do not be afraid" (John 6:19–20, my trans.). The phrase again appears when Jesus boldly states his existence before Abraham (John 8:57–58). During his arrest, he says the phrase, and the soldiers draw back and fall to the ground (John 18:5–6). During his trial, Jesus declares, "*Egō eimi*, and you will see the Son of Man seated at the right hand of power" (Mark 14:62, my trans.), prompting the high priest to accuse him of blasphemy. And earlier in his ministry, he looks forward to his resurrection and ascension and declares that on that day "you will know that *egō eimi*" (John 8:27–28, my trans.). Each of these examples comes across as abnormal, as if there is more than meets the eye when Jesus says, "*Egō eimi*."

This "I am" phrase is often traced to the famous scene in Exodus 3:14, where God declares his name to Moses: "I AM THAT I AM" (my trans.). But the phrasing in Exodus 3:14, both in the original Hebrew and in the Greek translation, includes a predicate, so it does not precisely match what Jesus says in the Gospels.[25]

An alternative source might consist of the statements that God makes elsewhere in the Old Testament that more closely match the *egō eimi* catchphrase, in both Hebrew and Greek.[26] For instance, God declares, "I am, and there is no god besides me" (Deut. 32:39, my trans.); or, "I, the LORD, the first and with the last: I am" (Isa. 41:4, my trans.); or, "Understand that I am—before me no god was formed, nor will there be any after me" (Isa. 43:10, my trans.). Several others from Isaiah could be added (43:25; 45:1–4, 18; 46:1–4; 48:12; 51:11–12). Significantly, each of these "I am" statements is spoken amid a strong claim of monotheism, whereby God asserts that he and only he is the true God.

Regardless of which Old Testament source is correct, Jesus's use of this formula is quite an impressive maneuver: with the predicate-less *egō eimi*, he is taking on his own lips some of the strongest wording used by YHWH to declare his uniqueness to ancient Israel.

If this is true, then it is not actually surprising that the New Testament authors read the Old Testament in such a compelling manner. Jesus pointed the way.

Summary

I began this chapter by introducing the conundrum facing early Christians: retaining strict monotheism *and* declaring Jesus

---

25. The Hebrew of Ex. 3:14 reads, *'ehyeh 'asher 'ehyeh*, which can be translated "I am what I am" or "I will be what I will be"; either way, the syntax does not match the Johannine phrase, although the second occurrence in the verse (*'ehyeh* by itself) comes closer. In the Greek translation of Ex. 3:14, the reading is *egō eimi ho ōn*, which is a predicate nominative that, again, does not match John.

26. The Hebrew form in these cases is *'ani hu'*, which is something like "I he" or "I am he," while the Greek form matches the New Testament phrase precisely.

Christ to be truly and fully God, all while avoiding polytheism. That is, they needed to avoid one extreme of presenting Jesus as just another "god" and another extreme of fully absorbing him into the Father in a flat kind of way (as in modalism).

They could have used Greek philosophy; they were certainly familiar with it (e.g., Acts 17:22–31). But they chose a better strategy. If you want to hold the tension of the full deity of the Son alongside strict monotheism, the most strategic source material is the Old Testament, which was the central authority for all Jews and early Christians.

Why? The Son of God manifested in the flesh of Jesus Christ can be considered really and truly God, in the way later formalized in the creeds, only if he is and always has been the "one God" of Israel disclosed in the Old Testament. He could not *become* this; he had to always be this. And that is precisely what the New Testament authors labor to convey in reading the Old Testament afresh in this direction. By applying Lord/*kyrios*, YHWH passages, divine prerogatives, divine metaphors, and the "I am" phrase to Jesus, the New Testament communicates this truth: he who is God in the Old Testament was, is, and always will be inclusive of the Son as the second person. There is no stronger way for a first-century Jesus follower to express all this than by the Wedgwood-like move of going straight to the Old Testament to do it.

So What?

In modern ecumenical discourse, a question regularly arises: Do Jews and Christians worship the same deity? It is understandably a very difficult question to answer, requiring much nuance and mutual respect.

On the one hand, the New Testament goes to great lengths to articulate how Christianity emerges from the root system of

Judaism (e.g., Rom. 11) and stands in continuity with ancient Israel in numerous ways (e.g., Gal. 3–4). If Abraham, Moses, David, and numerous others are deemed sharers of the same faith in God and eternal inheritance as Christians, then it is hard to give a firm no to the question.

On the other hand, this chapter has surveyed numerous lines of evidence that show, without a shadow of doubt, that the second person of the Godhead (the Son) is, in a complex way, *intrinsic to the God of ancient Israel.* Since a "flat" monotheism simply cannot square with the Old Testament or New Testament data and since modern Judaism denies the deity of the Son, it is just as hard to give a firm yes to the question.

If nothing else, the material surveyed in this chapter puts front and center how the monotheism of the (mostly Jewish) New Testament authors has been Christologically transformed. There is no way around the fact that, at least from an early Christian perspective, the God of ancient Israel necessarily includes the divine Son—and always has.

4

Maranatha

Early Worship of Christ

When our youngest child was two, we took a family trip to the North Carolina mountains. She had never seen them, so we spent a lot of time hyping them up. We also talked about how, when we got there, we would walk across a famous bridge that connects two mountain peaks. Thus, prior to the trip, we tried to give her as clear a concept as possible about mountains, heights, bridges, safety, and so forth.

When the trip came, she believed the right concepts. But when we approached the famous bridge, she had to make good on what she believed. The rubber was hitting the road: Would she walk on the bridge and trust it to hold her or not? It is one thing to believe ideas about bridge construction; it is another thing to put those beliefs into practice when you are looking at the chasm below.

The same is true when it comes to the divinity of Jesus Christ. So far we have covered three conceptual beliefs of early Christians: that he is eternally preexistent, that he stands in a unique relationship of oneness with the Father as God the Son, and that the Old Testament itself was interpreted to include Jesus Christ in the Godhead. But in many respects, the rubber hits the road with *behaviors*. Namely, did the early Christians make good on these ideas and actually *treat* Jesus as God? Or was it all just an intellectual exercise?

What I hope to show in this chapter is that yes, the earliest Christians acted on their beliefs by offering to Jesus full worship that belongs only to the one true God.[1] I examine five distinct worship patterns and then explore how the entire religious life of early Christians was understood as spiritually partaking in Christ. But first I must draw out an important clarification.

Christ the Intercessor in Worship

In recent decades, it has become common for some New Testament scholars to argue that Christ never *receives* true worship but rather that he is the one *through whom* the earliest Christians offer worship to God the Father.[2] The inference is

---

1. Seminal studies on the early church's worship of Jesus include Larry Hurtado, *Honoring the Son: Jesus in Earliest Christian Devotional Practice* (Bellingham, WA: Lexham, 2018); Hurtado, *How on Earth Did Jesus Become a God? Historical Questions about Earliest Devotion to Jesus* (Grand Rapids, MI: Eerdmans, 2005); Hurtado, *Lord Jesus Christ: Devotion to Jesus in Earliest Christianity* (Grand Rapids, MI: Eerdmans, 2003); Richard Bauckham, "The Worship of Jesus," in *The Climax of Prophecy: Studies on the Book of Revelation* (Edinburgh: T&T Clark, 1993), 174–98; Martin Hengel, "The Song about Christ in Earliest Worship," in *Studies in Early Christology* (Edinburgh: T&T Clark, 1995), 227–92. Consult these works (particularly those of Hurtado) for details on the patterns of religious observances in the ancient Mediterranean in general. While devotional practices, particularly in the context of the imperial cult, were quite diverse in the first century, it is clear that most Jews in that era categorically refused to participate in the veneration of local deities (see 1 Macc. 1–2). They reserved true acts of worship for the living God.
2. This is most strenuously argued in James D. G. Dunn, *Did the First Christians Worship Jesus? The New Testament Evidence* (London: SPCK, 2010).

then drawn that Christ is not quite fully divine but is simply the best possible mediator of the presence of God. The distinction is subtle, yes, but extremely important. If Jesus is simply a vessel through whom we worship God—and not someone we should worship *as God*—then all orthodox Trinitarianism unravels.

It is worth pausing, then, to clarify that the New Testament does indeed present Christ as an intermediary for Christians' acts of worship. He is, as Hebrews makes abundantly clear, the "great high priest" (Heb. 4:14) who goes into the heavenly tabernacle, where he saves those who "draw near to God through him" (Heb. 7:25). Moreover, Christ "intercedes" continually at the side of the Father (Rom. 8:34; Heb. 7:25), where he serves as the church's "advocate" (1 John 2:1) and prays on its behalf (John 14:16). Moreover, he is the "mediator between God and men" (1 Tim. 2:5), and it is "through" him or "in his name" that his followers offer prayers to God (John 16:23–24; Rom. 1:8; 7:25; Eph. 5:20; Col. 3:17).

Christ the Recipient of Worship

Without question, then, Christians offer religious devotion to God *through* Christ. He is the great intercessor in worship. But the question is this: Is he *more* than that? Does he also *receive* worship that is directed to him? Five specific patterns indicate that he is and he does.

Praying to Christ

Though later strands of Christianity (such as medieval Roman Catholicism) found it acceptable to address prayers to saints or Mary, this was unheard of among early Christians and ancient Israelites. Throughout the Old Testament, true worshipers of God never offer prayers to anyone other than God—not angels,[3] kings, or dead patriarchs. In fact, one of the key ways you know you are committing idolatry is by praying to false gods as if they were real (1 Kings 18:26–27; Isa. 45:20). God alone is the rightful recipient or addressee of prayer.

Thus, it is incredibly significant that the New Testament shows early Christians praying directly to Jesus Christ. An important (though debated) example is found in 1 Corinthians 16:22. Here Paul expresses in Aramaic what can be considered a brief prayer to Jesus: "*Marana-tha*," which may mean something like, "Our Lord, come!"[4] The immediate context indicates that Jesus is intended here, for in the next verse Paul refers to him as "*Lord* Jesus" (16:23). The fact that this brief prayer to Jesus is provided by Paul in Aramaic (while the rest of the epistle is Greek) shows that it likely goes back even earlier to the Aramaic-speaking followers of Jesus.

If this is indeed an early Christian prayer, then this devotional petition to the ascended Jesus is something no Jewish-background Christian would ever entertain unless he or she truly believed him to be God, who alone is the recipient of prayer.

Four other clear examples can be given. In Acts 1:24 the remaining apostles pray directly to the "Lord" to choose a replacement for Judas. Technically, "Lord" here could refer to the Father (recall chap. 3, above, on the fuzzy use of "Lord"). But given that the same apostles speak of "Lord Jesus" in 1:21 *and* that it was Jesus who had chosen the first twelve (and who chooses Paul in Acts 9), it is almost certain that Jesus is intended here.

---

3. Some Jewish writings depict angels serving as go-betweens in bringing prayers before God (1 En. 9.1–6; T. Levi 5.1–7; 4Q400–403), but they are not the *addressees* in prayer—God alone stands in that role.

4. Scholars debate whether it should be read as a prayer (as here) or a statement of fact (i.e., with a different vocalization, *Maran-atha*, "Our Lord has come"). Scholars have gone back and forth on this point, but (at least to the present author) the use of Aramaic (which would be unusual if Paul is simply stating a historical fact), the location of this phrase at the end of the letter (which is where Paul often inserts prayer formulas), and the parallel phrases in Rev. 22:20 and Did. 10.6 (see below) tilt the scales in the direction of *Marana-tha* being a prayer to Christ.

Later in Acts, as Stephen prepares to die, he prays to the one he sees standing in heaven: "Lord Jesus, receive my Spirit" (7:59). Furthermore, Paul describes how, when faced with the infamous "thorn" in his flesh, "three times [he] pleaded with the Lord," and the Lord answered his prayer as follows: "My grace is sufficient for you, for *my power* is made perfect in weakness" (2 Cor. 12:8–9). Once again, "Lord" here is fuzzy and could refer to the Father. But Paul clarifies that Jesus Christ is the one to whom he prayed—and the one who replied to his prayer—by referencing the *"power* of Christ" (12:9). Finally, in Revelation 22:20 the apostle John prays, "Come, Lord Jesus!" which likely echoes in Greek the aforementioned Aramaic *Marana-tha* prayer.

Each of these instances shows how early Christians (apostles, Stephen, Paul, John) prayed not only *through* but also *directly to* Jesus Christ, without giving any indication that they thought this was inappropriate. Where would they get the audacity to pray to Jesus as if he were God? Perhaps it was from Jesus himself, who exhorted them, "If you ask *me* anything in my name, I will do it" (John 14:14).[5] Jesus declared himself, along with the Father, to be the one who both receives and answers the prayers of his people.

Such a practice of praying to Jesus continues after the apostolic era. For instance, the same *Marana-tha* prayer to Christ appears in the Didache (10.6), where this petition forms the conclusion of an extended prayer that is to be used as part of the Lord's Supper. Ignatius writes, "If Jesus Christ, by your prayer, reckons me worthy,"[6] indicating that they should pray to Jesus and that he will respond. And Clement of Alexandria addresses a lengthy prayer, "O instructor, . . . Father, Charioteer of Israel, Son and Father, both in One."[7]

---

5. Not all manuscripts have "me" in John 14:14, but the earliest and best do.
6. Ignatius, *Eph.* 20.1.
7. Clement of Alexandria, *Paed.* 3.12.

Singing to Christ

As with prayer, singing was considered within the Old Testament and Judaism to be an act of worship that is directed only to God. Yet by AD 111, the Roman historian Pliny the Younger described to Emperor Trajan the worship pattern of early Christians as follows: "They were in the habit of meeting on a certain fixed day before it was light, when they sang in alternate verses a hymn to Christ, as to a god."[8] At least by the early second century, Christians were not only singing to God—as the people of Israel had always done—but singing *to Christ* as to God.

We see signs of this practice in the New Testament as well. Paul instructs the church to do the following: "Be filled with the Spirit, addressing one another in psalms and hymns and spiritual songs, singing and making melody *to the Lord*" (Eph. 5:18–19). "Lord" here could technically refer to God the Father, but Paul goes on in 5:20 to speak of "our Lord Jesus Christ," making clear that the "Lord" to whom Christians are to sing is the Son of God. Likewise (and more definitively), John reveals how the heavenly court "sang a new song, saying, 'Worthy are you . . . for you were slain'" (Rev. 5:9). The slain "you" to whom they are singing is clearly Jesus. In short, not only does the New Testament include songs that are *about* Jesus (such as the Magnificat and Benedictus of Luke 1), but it also features the practice of singing songs *to* him.

Venerating Christ in Ordinances

Every religious movement of the ancient world had ceremonies or ordinances done in honor of or to appease their deities. And the Israelites were no different, in that their entire sacrificial and ceremonial system was oriented around God. Of course, with the coming of Christ, these shadows faded as the reality appeared.

---

8. Pliny, *Letters* 10.96.

And thus, the system of sacrifices was replaced by spiritual worship in the New Testament era. Yet ordinances did not go away altogether in early Christianity. Two were mandated by Christ himself. What is fascinating is that the New Testament regularly speaks of both as being done "unto" or "in" the Lord Jesus.

Consider baptism as the initiating ordinance. Three times in Acts, the early Christians declare that one is baptized "in the name of" Jesus (Acts 2:38; 10:48; 19:5). This use of "name" is important, because to a Jewish-background Christian of this period, the "name" of God represents God himself.[9] Hence, being baptized "in" or "into" the name of Jesus expresses how such a washing is an actual act of worshiping him. Similarly, Paul writes of how we are "baptized into Christ Jesus" (Rom. 6:3–4). By leaving out the "name of" (found in Acts), he makes even clearer that the physical act of baptism somehow binds the confessing believer spiritually to Christ. What exactly the New Testament authors mean is hard to grasp; we will save the mystery of the sacrament for another day. But consider this thought experiment. What if someone said, "Be baptized in the name of Caesar" or "in the name of Napoleon" or "into the queen"? Regardless of one's religious perspective or high opinion of such individuals, such phrasing would either be incredibly odd or downright scandalous. Yet that is precisely what the early Christians said about Jesus Christ—early and often, and long before sacramental theology had fully developed. The inescapable conclusion is that early Christians could use such language only if they considered Jesus worthy of such exalted veneration.

The same is true of the sustaining ordinance of the Eucharist (or Holy Communion). Observe that the actual name given to it in the New Testament is the "Lord's Supper" (Gk. *kyriakon deipnon*, 1 Cor. 11:20). Jesus presides over it. It is *his* meal. It is

---

9. See especially Ex. 23:21; Num. 6:27; 1 Kings 8:29; 2 Chron. 7:16.

a means of fellowshipping with *him*, fulfilling both the Passover meal and the postsacrifice priestly meals of communion with God (e.g., Lev. 7:11–32). Paul further describes the Supper as "participation in the blood of Christ" and "participation in the body of Christ" (1 Cor. 10:16). What exactly he means continues to be debated, but it is clear that the ordinance somehow brings the worshiper into a kind of fellowship with the Lord Jesus in a way that is unparalleled by any other human meal (see John 6:53). But to stress how this sacrament is truly an act of worship of Christ, Paul goes on to compare it with Roman-era cultic meals that were a participation in the "cup of demons" and the "table of demons" (1 Cor. 10:21). What pagans do to worship false deities shares a similar pattern with the Lord's Supper, which is why the latter had to be handled so carefully at Corinth. It is not a mere meal but an act of worshiping Christ.

In addition to these primary ordinances, two other passages further display how early Christians saw Jesus as an appropriate recipient of acts of veneration. (1) Paul describes how Christians have liberty to choose to "observe" Jewish feast days or foods—provided they conduct such acts of worship "in honor of the Lord" (Rom. 14:6). Here "Lord" refers to Jesus, as Romans 14:8–9 makes clear. (2) Throughout the Old Testament, the "firstfruits" of any crop or livestock are offered to God and God only. In a subtle comment in Romans 16:5, Paul uses "firstfruits" (Gk. *aparchē*) as a metaphor for new believers and declares them "firstfruits to Christ" (my trans.). Thus, he subtly signals Christ to be a rightful recipient of the firstfruits, just as God is in the Old Testament era.

Calling on Christ in Ministry

Several times in the New Testament, Jesus's followers invoke him in distinct ways to enable their ministry. For instance, Paul appeals, almost as a kind of prayer, to both "our God and Father himself, and our Lord Jesus," that they might direct his path (1 Thess. 3:11) as well as comfort the afflicted church in Thessalonica (2 Thess. 2:16–17). Furthermore, early Christians regularly call on "the name of Jesus" or "the name of the Lord" to enable the lame to walk (Acts 3:6), to cast out demons (Acts 16:18), and to bring healing to the sick (James 5:14). In fact, "those who . . . call upon the name of our Lord Jesus Christ" becomes a kind of shorthand for Christians in 1 Corinthians 1:2.

Perhaps the most significant example is Paul's instruction about church discipline in 1 Corinthians 5:4–5. The context is corporate worship, when the Corinthians "are assembled in the name of the Lord Jesus" (5:4). Do not let this slip by unnoticed: the assembly for worship is *in the name of Jesus*. Christ sanctions it, and it is oriented around him. But Paul goes on to say that "with the power of our Lord Jesus," they are to turn a flagrantly unrepentant sinner out of their fellowship (5:4–5). In so doing, they are enacting the judgment of Jesus himself, not just human opinion, for Paul places all authority for this action on the "power" of Christ. This is intriguing, for Paul later appeals to the Old Testament for justification of such an action: namely, the authority of God (5:13, quoting Deut. 13:5 and similar passages). It is hard to imagine how Paul could invoke Jesus for church discipline in this way if he did not see him to be fully God.

Bowing Down in Worship

In historical dramas, servants are often portrayed bowing down to their superiors to show respect. If one were to use a Greek word for that verb of "bowing down," the primary option would be *proskynein*. Unfortunately, this word has a double use in first-century Greek: it is also regularly used for proper religious "worship" of God. So in the New Testament, one needs to be cautious when coming across this word.

For instance, in Matthew 18:26 a servant "bow[s] down" (Gk. *prosekynei*, my trans.) before his master to beg his patience as he tries to pay down his debt. In no sense is this servant "worshiping" his master. But this same verb is used in the Gospels for a variety of people who approach Jesus and "bow down" before him. English translations often vary in translating instances of *proskynein* with either "bow down" (as a sign of respect) or "worship" (in a religious way). Not all of them need be understood as a sign of authentic, religious veneration of Jesus. But some should be.[10]

Let us work backward from the end of the New Testament. Revelation describes the heavenly hosts circling around the throne "before the Lamb" and falling on their faces to "worship" (Rev. 7:9–12). In this magnificent scene, the object of their worship is both God the Father and God the Lamb (Son), who are reigning *together* on one throne (7:17). But the worship of Christ is even clearer in Revelation 5:13–14, where it says that the angels and elders "fell down and worshiped" the Lamb. Hebrews echoes the same sense when it records that God commands the angels to "worship" the Son (Heb. 1:6). It is stunning that the New Testament describes how not only humans but also angels are to worship Jesus. This heavenly worship (using *proskynein*) of Jesus Christ is one of the most obvious indications of the early Christian view of his full divinity.

But such worship is not confined to heaven. At the end of his earthly ministry, Jesus offers final instructions to his

---

10. For an extended discussion of this topic, see Ray M. Lozano, *The* Proskynesis *of Jesus in the New Testament: A Study on the Significance of Jesus as an Object of* προσκυνέω *in the New Testament Writings*, LNTS 609 (London: T&T Clark, 2020).

disciples and ascends into glory. Luke records how, *after this*, the disciples "worshiped him and returned to Jerusalem with great joy" (Luke 24:52). The context makes it clear that a mere act of bowing to pay respect cannot be intended by *proskynein* here, for such a show of respect from inferior to superior requires the superior to be present; one does not bow down or curtsy for a superior not in the room. But here *Jesus is no longer on the scene*. He has gone into heaven. So the only option for *proskynein* is that the disciples are truly worshiping him as God.

A few days earlier, the resurrected Jesus is greeted twice by his followers, who "fall at his feet" and "worship" him (Matt. 28:9, 17, my trans.). Though it is possible that this could simply be a sign of respect for their no-longer-dead rabbi, it is worth noting that this combination appears elsewhere in the New Testament. John "[falls] down" at the feet of an angel and attempts to "worship" him (Rev. 19:10; 22:8–9), and Cornelius does the same to Peter (Acts 10:25–26). But in these instances, the angel and Peter emphatically reject their attempts to worship (Gk. *proskynein*) them—showing that their action is not merely a neutral sign of respect but religious veneration reserved only for God.[11] Jesus, on the other hand, does not appear the least bit uncomfortable when the same thing happens to him. The evidence is not decisive, but viewed in light of the other data, it seems that these encounters in Matthew 28 do constitute religious worship of Jesus, which he does not reject.

Two earlier scenes stand out as possible (but not definitive) instances where people offer real worship to Jesus even before

---

11. For an extensive survey of the early evidence for how angels refuse attempted acts of worship, see Loren Stuckenbruck, *Angel Veneration and Christology: A Study in Early Judaism and in the Christology of the Apocalypse of John*, WUNT, 2nd ser., vol. 70 (Tübingen: Mohr Siebeck, 1995). The instances where angels reject human attempts to worship them make the worship of Jesus stand out all the more.

his resurrection: (1) the disciples who "worship" him in the boat and acclaim him to be "the Son of God" after he walks on water (Matt. 14:33) and (2) the blind man who confesses belief in Jesus and then "worships" him (John 9:38).

This brings us to the earliest episode where the verb *proskynein* is directed to Jesus: the visit of the magi. In Matthew 2:2 these visitors state their desire to "worship" (Gk. *proskynein*) in his presence, and then in 2:11 they make good on it when they find the boy. Given that their stated purpose is to bring gifts to the one "who has been born king of the Jews" (2:2), it is possible they are only paying respect to a new ruler.

We must keep in mind, however, that Matthew's birth story has already identified this newborn Jesus as "Immanuel," conceived by the Holy Spirit (1:23). And as shown above, Matthew includes other scenes in the Gospel where actual religious worship of Jesus is almost certainly happening. So is the evangelist making a subtle use of *proskynein* with the magi—for those who have ears to hear? Possibly. At the end of the Gospel narrative, Jesus claims to have "all authority in heaven and on earth" and sends his disciples out to "all nations" (28:18–19). This global emphasis, however, begins all the way back in Matthew 2:2, where the Persian magi symbolically represent "all nations" coming to acknowledge the authority of the newborn king. Perhaps Matthew is implying that, whether they know it or not, these magi "bowing down" to Jesus are in fact doing the right thing: *worshiping* the sovereign king over all things, who is Immanuel.

The Christian Life as "Union with Christ"

In each of the five preceding subsections, I have outlined a distinct action among early followers of Jesus, and when all are combined, they provide a very clear portrait of how early

Christians not only worshiped through him (as intercessor) but worshiped him directly in the same way they would worship God. But we can add one more layer.

After Jesus's ascension, the church begins expressing, essentially overnight, the shocking idea that Christians are somehow—in a real way that remains perplexing even today—*united* to Christ. That is, the worship and devotional life of early Christians is characterized not just by prayers and songs to Jesus (among other things) but by a deeply significant *communing* with him or *abiding* in him. Mysteriously, across time (thousands of years), space (heaven and earth), and geography (nations everywhere), all Christians are united to the risen Christ in a way that lacks parallel in any known religious system ever. Several features of this phenomenon merit attention.[12]

I begin with Jesus himself. When on the Damascus Road he apocalyptically appears from heaven to Paul—who, recall, was hunting down Christians—he says, "Why are you persecuting me?" (Acts 9:4; repeated in 22:7; 26:14). This is a curious way to phrase it, for Paul cannot, strictly speaking, persecute Jesus himself when Jesus is enthroned in heaven. Rather, Paul is persecuting Jesus's followers. But Jesus himself says that they are "me" in some profound way. When Paul attacks Christians, he is attacking Jesus. Jesus, in other words, *incorporates* his followers in himself. This is simply another way of expressing what Jesus had already told his disciples, namely, that he is the vine and they are the branches (John 15:5).

Paul builds on this concept in his letters. He describes again and again how all Christians are intimately connected across

---

12. For more details on the Christological implications of union with Christ, see Chris Tilling, *Paul's Divine Christology* (Grand Rapids, MI: Eerdmans, 2015). To learn more about the broader theme of union with Christ in Paul, see Constantine R. Campbell, *Paul and Union with Christ: An Exegetical and Theological Study* (Grand Rapids, MI: Zondervan, 2012).

space-time with the historical saving work of Jesus: we died and were buried "with him" (Rom. 6:4–8; Gal. 2:20; 2 Tim. 2:11); we are raised "with him" (Col. 2:12; 3:1; cf. Rom. 6:11); we are exalted "with him" (Eph. 2:6); in fact, before creation we are elect "in him" (Eph. 1:4). All salvation stems from being united "in/with" the saving things Jesus did.

This connection that Christians have to Christ blossoms with a variety of other descriptions of how we are in him and he is in us. We are the "body" of Christ (Rom. 12:5; 1 Cor. 12:12), and Christ is our "head" (1 Cor. 11:3; Eph. 4:15; 5:23). We are nourished by Christ (John 6:35, 51; Eph. 5:29; Col. 2:19). Our lives in the present are "hidden with Christ in God" (Col. 3:3). And, amazingly, Christ is "in" us as well (Rom. 8:10; Col. 1:27)—which is precisely as Jesus had prayed, "I in them . . . that they may become perfectly one" (John 17:23). Put differently, there are two dimensions to the Christian life: "We abide in him and he in us" (1 John 4:13).

Indeed, Jesus concludes his ministry with the promise that, though enthroned in heaven, he will be "with [his followers] always, to the end of the age" (Matt. 28:20)—echoing God's "Immanuel" promise throughout the Old Testament to "be with" his people.

No mere human could claim such things, and no sane people could ever say such things about their relationship with an ordinary man. What on earth would it mean to be nourished by, engrafted into, united with, or "in" a mere human prophet or king? The only close Old Testament parallel to this sense of the real presence of the exalted Christ is the spiritual relationship the Israelites share with God himself. Only a divine being who transcends creation can have this kind of relationship of mutual indwelling with his worshipers across time and place.

Summary

In this chapter I have attempted to outline the evidence for how the early followers of Jesus afforded him the kind of religious worship reserved for God alone.

Perhaps this veneration of Jesus explains why the early Christian movement was so strongly disliked by opponents. On the Jewish side of the aisle, the Christians were kicked out of the synagogue (John 12:42) and subjected to intense suffering (1 Thess. 2:13–16). This level of antagonism seems to go beyond a mere intramural disagreement about Jesus's messianic status. Before his conversion, Paul even sought the death of Christians (Acts 22:4). Why would he do this unless their religious offenses were worthy of the death penalty? At that time, would the belief that some dead rabbi had been resurrected have been such an offense? Likely not. Rather, Paul explains that he wanted to destroy them because they called on the name of Jesus (Acts 9:14; 26:9), suggesting that he thought they were violating the veneration of the "name" of God (as expressed in the third commandment, Ex. 20:7).

On the Greek side of the aisle, Paul was (after his conversion) accused not only of preaching nonsense about a resurrected Messiah but, more specifically, of preaching "foreign divinities" (Acts 17:18). Some Roman critics would eventually accuse early Christians of being *a*theists(!) for their refusal to venerate the local pagan deities because of their exclusive worship of Christ.[13]

In short, it seems that the early Christians provoked such strong reactions in their contemporaries not only because of their *conceptual* claims about Jesus but because they actually *acted on them* by worshiping Christ in a real way. This act was, indeed, the greater line in the sand—and the greater offense.

---

13. This dynamic lies behind the worship of the image of the beast in Rev. 13–14.

So What?

New Christians often ask, "Should I pray just to the Father or to the Son as well?" While Jesus does model for us prayer to the Father, especially in the Lord's Prayer ("Our Father in heaven . . . ," Matt. 6:9), it is also clear that early Christian practice was to direct prayer to the Son as well. While modern Christians often appear more comfortable singing songs *about* Jesus and his work, one wonders whether we might need to regain a sense of offering full worship to the Son alongside the Father.

Moreover, the real spiritual union Christians have with the risen and ascended Lord Jesus should stimulate more precise reflection on the nature of the Christian life. It is not so much that we should ask ourselves, "What would Jesus do?" or even pursue a "personal walk with Jesus" (though each of those phrases contains an element of truth). Rather, we should see the Christian life as one in which Jesus, who abides in us by his Spirit, is producing the obedience of faith from within us, as the outflow of a renewed heart. By uniting you to himself, Jesus molds you into conformity with himself through Christ-shaped worship in all of life. *That* is a vision for the Christian life that takes seriously the union we have with the Lord Jesus.

5

Three Persons

Trinitarian Relations in Full Color

Muhammad records a somewhat perplexing comment in the
Qur'an: "Beware the Day when Allah will say, 'O Jesus, Son of
Mary, did you say to the people, "Take me and my mother as
deities besides Allah"?'" (Q Ma'ida 5:116). This passage joins
a few others (Q Baqara 2:163; Q Ma'ida 5:72; Q Nahl 16:51;
Q Qasas 28:88) that convey the standard Islamic teaching
about the absolute oneness of Allah and the nondivine nature
of Jesus. But this *sūrah* goes further by condemning the notion
of *three* divine figures—only with a twist. The alleged "Trinity"
that Muhammad opposes (elsewhere he commands, "Say not
Three," Q Nisa' 4:171) is confusedly made up of Allah, Jesus,
and Mary.

Today this doctrine remains a major dividing point between
Christianity and Islam, but the interesting thing is that Muhammad, for all his denial of the divinity of Jesus, appears aware

that Christianity claims something more than just a divine Jesus Christ. And he is right about that.

So far I have traced the various lines of evidence supporting the claim that the New Testament does, indeed, teach the full divinity of Jesus. But Christianity is not *bi*nitarian. We cannot simply confess Jesus to be God without also embracing the fullness of a *triune* God. Sadly, although Muhammad had some awareness that there is a third person in the Christian Godhead (but misidentified that person's identity), many within Christian circles today do not understand the basics of this foundational doctrine. The proper third person of the Godhead—the Holy Spirit—is often seen to be a life force or a kind of impersonal gas that fills the atmosphere in a worship service or a power to do amazing things.

The aim of this chapter, then, is to bring this third person more fully into the discussion and demonstrate that the New Testament teaches not only that Jesus Christ is fully God but that he is divine in a particular way. Namely, he is the Son in eternal relation to both the Father *and the Spirit*, and the three persons are fully one God. In other words, any discussion of a divine Christ must necessarily factor in the divine Spirit, or else it is woefully incomplete.

The Personhood of the Spirit

Before proceeding, it is important to survey the evidence that indicates that the Holy Spirit is, indeed, a divine *person* and not just something akin to "the Force" of the Jedi. While Scripture never provides an elaborate treatise on the personhood of the Spirit, the authors *treat* the Spirit as a person throughout.

First, the Holy Spirit is regularly the subject of verbs that are only ever done by actual willing, thinking, active *persons*. These activities are never done by wind, ideas, inanimate forces, gases, or anything of the sort. The Spirit does the following in the New Testament:

- appoints (Gk. *tithenai*, Acts 20:28)
- bears witness / testifies (Gk. *martyrein*, Acts 20:23; Heb. 10:15; 1 John 5:6; cf. 5:32)
- deems something good (Gk. *dokein*, Acts 15:28)
- forbids (Gk. *kōlyein*, Acts 16:6)
- gives life (Gk. *zōopoiein*, John 6:63)
- gives new birth (Gk. *gennan*, John 3:8)
- guides (Gk. *hodēgein*, John 16:13)
- intercedes in prayer (Gk. *hyperentynchanein*, Rom. 8:26–27)
- predicts the future (Gk. *promartyresthai*, 1 Pet. 1:11)
- searches the mind (Gk. *eraunan*, 1 Cor. 2:10–11)
- speaks (Gk. *lalein* and *legein*, Matt. 10:20; Mark 13:11; Acts 1:16; 8:29; 11:12; 13:2; Heb. 3:7)
- teaches (Gk. *didaskein*, John 14:26)
- wills/decrees certain things (Gk. *boulesthai*, 1 Cor. 12:7–11)

Second, humans do things to the Spirit that are done only to real persons, such as lying to the Spirit (Acts 5:3–9), blaspheming the Spirit (Matt. 12:31), and resisting the Spirit (Acts 7:51).

For the New Testament authors to conceive of the Spirit *doing* these things or of these things *being done* to the Spirit, they must have believed the Spirit to be a real, albeit spiritual, person.[1]

---

1. A third argument has occasionally been made in support of the personhood of the Spirit: the apparent use of the masculine pronoun *ekeinos* for the Spirit in John 16:13–14, whereas normally in Greek the word for Spirit (*pneuma*) is neuter. While this argument appears sound at first—namely, that the Spirit is "he" in this passage—it is not ultimately compelling. *Ekeinos* here is almost certainly taking "Comforter" (which is masculine) as its referent. For details, see Andrew David Naselli and Philip R. Gons, "Prooftexting the Personality of the Holy Spirit: An Analysis of the Masculine Demonstrative Pronouns in John 14:26, 15:26, and 16:13–14," *DBTJ* 16 (2011): 65–89.

Let us proceed, then, to look closely at how the New Testament rounds out our understanding of the divinity of Jesus by painting him in triune colors, bringing the person of the Spirit into the discussion.

Triune Relations in Jesus's Ministry

I start out with the earthly Jesus. As detailed in chapter 2, the New Testament evidence is decisive that his unique eternal relationship of Son to Father is essential to who he is. But let us not overlook his intimate relationship to the Holy Spirit.[2]

Two of the Gospels begin by describing an unrepeatable, supernatural singularity: the conception of Jesus "by" or "from" the Holy Spirit (Matt. 1:18–20; Luke 1:35). Though the human mind continues to be baffled as to *how* this happened, early Christians were united in confessing that the Spirit is the divine agent of the conception of the Son, from Luke (who described it as an "overshadowing" of Mary by the Spirit) to the Nicene and Apostles' Creeds.

Three decades later, the Gospels record, Jesus's inauguration to public ministry is met not only with the voice of the Father from heaven but also with descent of the Holy Spirit on him (Matt. 3:16; Mark 1:10; Luke 3:22; John 1:32). Indeed, the entire scene is richly Trinitarian: the Son addresses the Father in prayer (Luke 3:21), the Father speaks to the Son, and the Father sends the Spirit on the Son. Subsequently, it is the Spirit who leads Jesus into the wilderness and sustains

---

2. For detailed studies of the Trinitarian relations in the Gospels, see Brandon D. Crowe and Carl R. Trueman, eds., *The Essential Trinity: New Testament Foundations and Practical Relevance* (Phillipsburg, NJ: P&R, 2017); Andreas J. Köstenberger and Scott R. Swain, *Father, Son and Spirit: The Trinity and John's Gospel*, NSBT 24 (Downers Grove, IL: InterVarsity Press, 2008); C. Kavin Rowe, "Luke and the Trinity: An Essay in Ecclesial Biblical Theology," *SJT* 56, no. 1 (2003): 1–26; M. M. B. Turner, "Luke and the Spirit: Studies in the Significance of Receiving the Spirit in Luke-Acts" (PhD diss., University of Cambridge, 1980).

him during temptation (Matt. 4:1; Mark 1:12; Luke 4:1, 14) through the word of his Father (Matt. 4:4; Luke 4:4). And when Jesus preaches in Nazareth, he declares himself to be anointed by the Holy Spirit (Luke 4:18), who is specifically "of the Lord GOD" in the Isaiah 61 passage he is citing. In short, the launch of Jesus's ministry is thoroughly saturated with both Spirit and Father.

And it does not stop there. Jesus casts out demons by the Spirit (Matt. 12:28). Moreover, revisiting a passage discussed in chapter 2, we find that the so-called Johannine thunderbolt (Luke 10:21–22) is vibrantly Trinitarian: the Son "rejoice[s] in the Holy Spirit" and then addresses his Father about their mutual "knowing." Finally, in an astounding scene prior to Jesus's ascension, he speaks of how he is going back to his Father and thus is sending out his apostles "as the Father has sent [him]" (John 20:21). Then he "breathe[s]" on them and says, "Receive the Holy Spirit" (John 20:22). In this profoundly Trinitarian way, Jesus passes the torch: the Father sent the Son, and the Son sends the apostles and consecrates them by breathing the Spirit on them—the same Spirit who had come on *him* at the inauguration of his ministry years earlier.

No doubt, others possess the Spirit in the New Testament, such as John the Baptist (Luke 1:15) and Simeon (Luke 2:25). But things are exponentially different for Jesus. A profound relation with the Spirit and Father defines the essence of who Jesus is and what he does from conception onward. It is no exaggeration to say that Jesus's earthly identity and ministry cannot be understood in any other way than thoroughly Trinitarian. What makes this all the more compelling is how the Gospel authors never stop to *explain* the Trinity—they just assume it.

Triune Relations at Pentecost

This Father-Son-Spirit relational identity of Jesus is manifested after his ascension as well, particularly at Pentecost. Let us rewind the tape and play it forward from the Old Testament.

Before and during Israel's exile, God promises numerous times to send his Spirit as the decisive sign that the eschatological era—the last days of restoration—has arrived (e.g., Isa. 44:3; 59:21; Ezek. 36:27). The clearest prophecy of the coming Spirit is found in Joel 2:28–29, where YHWH promises, "In those days I will pour out my Spirit." It is *his* Spirit, and he is the one who will pour out the Spirit. Hold that thought.

When Jesus comes on the scene, his forerunner, John the Baptist, promises well ahead of time that *Jesus* will send the Spirit (Matt. 3:11; Mark 1:8). But later in his ministry Jesus asks *the Father* to send the Spirit (John 14:16). Yet after his resurrection, Jesus promises that *he himself* will send the Spirit but describes this as "the promise of my Father" (Luke 24:49; Acts 1:4). So in a kind of tennis match, the ball goes back and forth as to who exactly is sending the Spirit: Father or Son? Essentially, the answer is yes. Jesus gives voice to this very dynamic in John 15:26: "When the Helper comes, whom I send to you from the Father, the Spirit of truth, who comes forth from the Father, he will bear witness about me" (my trans.). The Spirit is "sent" by Jesus but "comes forth" from the Father, and the Spirit in turn "witnesses" to Jesus. This statement expresses as closely as possible the beautiful web of interrelations between Father and Son, Father and Spirit, and Son and Spirit.[3]

---

3. One of the most divisive church controversies in the wake of the Council of Nicaea revolved around the *Filioque* (Lat. "and the Son") clause of the creed: Does the Holy Spirit "proceed" from the Father alone, or from the Father "and the Son"? This debate factored into the broader split of the church into East and West.

The fulfillment of all this takes place at Pentecost. John states that the gift of the Spirit hinges on the glorification of Jesus (John 7:39), and this is precisely how things play out in Acts: very soon after Jesus's ascent, the Holy Spirit is poured out as the eschatological sign that announces the arrival of the era of restoration (Acts 2:1–41). In his famous sermon, Peter appeals to the aforementioned passage from Joel 2:28–29, which reminds the Jewish audience that *God* had promised to send the Spirit in the latter days. But Peter gives a fuller revelation of what Joel is about: "This Jesus, . . . exalted at the right hand of God, and having received from the Father the promise of the Holy Spirit, he has poured out this that you yourselves are seeing and hearing" (Acts 2:32–33). Put differently, that which is the prerogative of YHWH in Joel and the prerogative of the Father in Acts 1:4 is now exercised by the ascended Son. The Father promised he would do it; then he gives the Spirit to the Son, who, upon receiving the Spirit, in turn pours out the Spirit.

Not only is this a significant claim to Jesus's divinity— where he exercises an exclusive prerogative of God (see chap. 3, above)—but it also helps provide some color to the triune relations among Father, Son, and Spirit. The Father's promise to send the Holy Spirit is both contingent on (John 7:39) and fulfilled by (Acts 2:32–33) the exalted Son.

Triune Relations and the Essence of God

As seen so far, the Spirit is essential to understanding Jesus's earthly ministry and Pentecost. Venturing beyond the Gospels and Acts, I focus on a few key examples where the Trinitarian relations shine through in full color.[4]

---

4. For detailed studies of the Trinity in Paul's writings, see Wesley Hill, *Paul and the Trinity: Persons, Relations, and the Pauline Letters* (Grand Rapids, MI: Eerdmans, 2015);

First, Paul picks up where Jesus left off by reiterating how the Spirit belongs to or proceeds from *both* the Father and the Son. Paul writes that the "Spirit of [God's] Son" is indeed "sent" by the Father (Gal. 4:6). He also speaks in Romans 15:19 of the "Spirit of God" (i.e., the Father, in context) and in 2 Corinthians 3:17 of the "Spirit of the Lord" (i.e., Christ, in context). This culminates in Romans 8:9, where in the same breath he speaks of "the Spirit of God" and "the Spirit of Christ." The Spirit is "of" both.

Second, these mutual relations are also central to redemptive actions in the past. Looking to Israel's history, Peter asserts that the salvation that is from God (i.e., the Father, in context) was communicated to the prophets by the "Spirit of Christ," enabling them to predict the "sufferings of Christ" (1 Pet. 1:5, 11). In other words, the Trinity is both the giver of revelation to the Old Testament prophets and the content of that revelation. Looking to the events of Christ's life, Paul speaks of the bodily resurrection of the "Son" by the Father to be "according to the Spirit" (Rom. 1:4). And looking to the apostolic era, the "Spirit of God" enables Paul to fulfill the "gospel of Christ" in his itinerant ministry from Jerusalem to Illyricum (Rom. 15:19). In short, when it comes to objective actions in history, none of the three divine persons is an island to himself. Each always exists and acts with the others in view.

Third, the three persons in some way participate in one another's identity. This concept is hard to express, for human analogies always fail to capture it. But a few passages give us a taste. According to Paul, they share in oneness: "one Spirit . . . one Lord . . . one God" (Spirit, Son, Father, respectively; Eph. 4:4–6). They also mysteriously share in existence: in a discus-

---

Francis Watson, "The Triune Divine Identity: Reflections on Pauline God-Language, in Disagreement with J. D. G. Dunn," *JSNT* 23, no. 80 (2001): 99–124.

sion about how Christians are to be transformed into the image of Christ, Paul twice states that "the Lord *is* the Spirit" (2 Cor. 3:17, 18). Most impressive is Romans 8:11. The intricacy of his Greek phrasing is hard to capture in English. I use numerical labels below to help track the divine persons (1 = Father, 2 = Son, 3 = Spirit):

> If the [3] Spirit of [1] the one who raised [2] Jesus from the dead dwells in you, [1] the one who raised [2] Jesus from the dead will also give life to your mortal bodies through [1] his [3] Spirit who dwells in you. (my trans.)

Notice that the divine persons appear seven times in succession. The Spirit is the one indwelling, and the Father is the one who is giving life. Strikingly, the Father is not even named directly, neither as "Father" nor as "God." Instead, his identity in this sequence is captured in a participial phrase—"the one who raised." Furthermore, his identity is tied to Jesus (whom he raised) *and* to the Spirit (whom he sends to indwell Christians). The Spirit is "of" the Father and is "his." And the Son is defined as the one raised by the Father. It is simply marvelous. In this compact phrase, Paul has welded the identities of each divine person fully with the others. They retain their distinctions, but they are fully and truly one. A more Trinitarian way of thinking could scarce be found.

Finally, one must not overlook what are often deemed the two most explicit affirmations of the Trinity in the New Testament. First, prior to his ascension, Jesus famously specifies that baptism must be done "in the name of the Father and of the Son and of the Holy Spirit" (Matt. 28:19). It is not "the names" (plural), nor is "name" repeated each time ("the name of . . . the name of . . . the name of"). Rather, a singular "the name" is shared across all three divine persons. The single "name" that bears with it the authority and presence of God is jointly shared by all three persons of the one Godhead.

Second, the other example is the so-called Johannine Comma of 1 John 5:7. It is one of the most debated textual variants in the Greek New Testament. The KJV reads, "For there are three that bear record in heaven, the Father, the Word, and the Holy Ghost: and these three are one." Quite understandably such a verse has been treated as *the* decisive Trinity proof text in the New Testament.[5] Nearly all other English translations outside the KJV tradition, however, omit it, because a lot of manuscript evidence suggests that the sentence was added later and is not original to John's epistle.[6] But if this chapter accomplishes nothing else, it certainly lays to rest any concerns over losing theological ground if 1 John 5:7 is inauthentic. Without it, still numerous other data points clearly teach a Trinitarian conception of God. Adding this verse does not move the needle much. A better way of treating it is this: the addition of the verse by a later scribe shows beyond a shadow of a doubt that the early church agreed that God is three-in-one. Where did such a scribe get this idea? From the rest of the New Testament!

In short, the cumulative force of the material in this section establishes one truth: though the term *Trinity* does not appear in the New Testament, the concept is there. While the New Testament regularly speaks of each divine person in distinct ways, not one of them can be fully understood without the others. Their identities *constitute* one another. Divine oneness is forged by their relations to each other. The creeds eventually come to express this by describing the Father as unbegotten, the Son as begotten of the Father, and the Spirit as proceeding from the

---

5. The Westminster Confession of Faith, for instance, cites it in the original proof texts for chap. 2 (given that the divines used the KJV, or Authorized Version).

6. The historical backstory of the Johannine Comma is complicated and cannot be easily summarized here.

Father and the Son. But the raw material is there on the pages of the New Testament from the earliest days.

Summary

What I have attempted to show in this chapter is that we cannot speak simply of a "divine Christ." There is no such thing as "binitarian Christology." Even the term "Christological monotheism" does not quite cut it. The New Testament does not stop at affirming that Jesus is God (Muhammad got that part right). Rather, it teaches that Jesus is God specifically in a Trinitarian way: as the Son of the Father and as the one who also stands in complex relation to the divine Spirit (not Mary—Muhammad got *that* part wrong). Perhaps the most satisfactory label is "Trinitarian Christology."

If all this is true, then an interesting thing happens when one examines what it means to be a Christian in light of the Trinitarian Christology covered in this chapter. Picking up the thread from the end of chapter 4, I would argue that the New Testament speaks of the Christian experience of salvation and worship not only as Christological (union with Christ) but also as deeply Trinitarian.

In terms of personal salvation, the Father, Son, and Spirit are jointly working throughout the spiritual progression of a Christian:

- foreknown by the Father, in the holiness of the Spirit, unto obedience to Christ (1 Pet. 1:2)
- taught spiritual truths for salvation by Father, Son, and Spirit (1 Cor. 2:10–16; Eph. 1:17)
- regenerated by the Spirit, who is sent by the Father through Jesus Christ (Titus 3:4–6)
- enabled to confess Christ's lordship by the Spirit of God (1 Cor. 12:3)

- washed, sanctified, and justified in the name of Jesus and by the Spirit of God (1 Cor. 6:11)
- adopted as children of God, made coheirs with Christ, enabled to pray to God—all by the Spirit (Rom. 8:15–17, 27)
- brought near by Christ and given access to God through the Spirit (Eph. 2:17–18)
- provided with gifts by the Spirit, the Lord, and God (1 Cor. 12:4–6)
- sustained by the grace of Christ, the love of God, and the fellowship of the Spirit (2 Cor. 13:14)

From start to finish, the individual Christian life is one of fellowship with the triune God.

The corporate life of worship is likewise conceived in Trinitarian terms. Paul describes the church as a "letter of Christ" written by the "Spirit of the living God" (2 Cor. 3:3, my trans.). He speaks of how the church of God was obtained by the blood of the Son and is sustained by leaders given by the Spirit (Acts 20:28). The church is God's temple indwelled by the Spirit (1 Cor. 3:16; "you" is plural here), and Christians are those who "worship by the Spirit of God and glory in Christ Jesus" (Phil. 3:3).

In sum, not only did the earliest Christians *conceptualize* the Godhead as three persons constituting one God, but their personal and corporate religious *experience* of God was fully Trinitarian as well. Thus, merely saying, "Yes, the New Testament teaches that Jesus is God," is good—but not sufficient. We must ensure we know and experience his divine essence in a specifically Trinitarian way that does not bracket out the Spirit.

So What?

Christians often speak of a "personal walk with Christ." However, the material in this chapter suggests that the Father and

Spirit might be neglected by such a truncated view. We cannot "walk" with Christ without walking with the triune God in his fullness. We cannot, for instance, merely "ask Jesus into our hearts" without acknowledging that this happens by the Holy Spirit, since the resurrected Jesus is in heaven at the right hand of the Father. For many, the Trinity is just a doctrine, and the Spirit in particular is often neglected. But properly speaking, the Trinity should be an enriching reality that shapes how one lives.

"My Lord and My God"

Calling Jesus *Theos*

Is Jesus ever actually called "God" in the Bible?

Some claim that the answer to this question is no, which is considered the smoking gun about the nondivine nature of Jesus by skeptics, Jehovah's Witnesses, unitarians, and the like. But this is an overly hasty and simplistic conclusion.

As mentioned at the outset, answering this question is quite tricky. Elsewhere in the ancient world and in Scripture, the Greek word *theos* is used not only for the true "God" but also for lesser beings that are labeled "god." Thus, simply calling someone *theos* is not necessarily a claim to full divine status.

This is precisely why I did not begin with this question but have saved it for now. In the preceding chapters, I covered numerous lines of evidence showing that the early Christians *describe* and *treat* Jesus Christ as fully God, in the way articulated in the orthodox creeds. Such evidence would carry the day, regardless of the answer to the question behind this chapter.

Yet in this chapter, I show that the answer to this question is not even *no* to begin with. In seven reasonably certain instances and five debated instances, the New Testament does directly apply *theos* to Jesus. As I survey them, the reader is encouraged to keep in mind all the prior evidence, which clarifies what the New Testament authors actually mean when they call Jesus "God": he is not a lesser "god" but *the* "God" of Israel. These explicit instances are simply icing on the cake.[1]

Seven Clear Instances

Let us begin with seven cases where there is relatively little debate that *theos* is predicated of Jesus. A fair warning must be given before wading into this topic: some of what follows involves grammatical heavy lifting. The payoff, however, should be worth it. (Note: all biblical translations in this section are my own.)

Titus 2:13 and 2 Peter 1:1

Both Titus 2:13 and 2 Peter 1:1 feature the same pattern, whereby "God" and "Savior" are used to describe Jesus. In Greek the article "the" (*ho*) appears before "God"—even though we do not generally translate it in English—but not before "Savior." In effect, this single use of the article with both "God" and "Savior" glues the two together into one designation, which is then applied to Jesus. I will try to capture this meaning with a wooden translation (setting "the" [Gk. *ho*] in bold):

> appearing of the glory of **the** great *theos* and Savior of us, Jesus Christ (Titus 2:13)

---

1. In what follows, I am drawing on a variety commentaries and advanced Greek grammars; there are few consolidated discussions of all these verses. Several are covered in the appendix of Raymond E. Brown, *An Introduction to New Testament Christology* (Mahwah, NJ: Paulist, 1994).

in the righteousness of the *theos* of us and Savior, Jesus
Christ (2 Pet. 1:1)

Some argue that "of us" in 2 Peter 1:1, which appears after
"God" rather than after "Savior" (as in Titus 2:13), breaks
up the logic and separates the two designations from one
another. While this is theoretically possible, Peter does the
same thing a few verses later: "**the** Lord *of us* and Savior,
Jesus Christ" (2 Pet. 1:11). Here "of us" stands between
"Lord" and "Savior," but the two terms are still referring
to the same person, Jesus. So there is no reason to assume
otherwise for 1:1.

The grammatical principle at play here is called the "Granville Sharp Rule," which has generated no small amount of
debate. The more disputed possible examples of the rule include Ephesians 5:5 ("the kingdom of **the** Christ and *theos*");
2 Thessalonians 1:12 ("the grace of **the** *theos* of us and Lord
Jesus Christ"); and 1 Timothy 5:21 and 2 Timothy 4:1 (both
of which read, "the presence of **the** *theos* and Christ Jesus").
They are thus excluded from consideration here. Very few,
however, dispute that the rule applies to Titus 2:13 and
2 Peter 1:1.

In short, it is fairly clear that Paul and Peter apply a joint
designation—something like "the *theos* and Savior of us"—
to Jesus. And thus they are calling him "God."

Hebrews 1:8

The preexistence angle of Hebrews 1:8 was covered in chapter 1, so here I focus on its use of *theos*. Recall that the writer
quotes the Old Testament several times, and in Hebrews 1:8 he
describes how God (the Father) is speaking directly to the Son
in Psalm 45:7 (the quoted portion), as follows:

But to the Son, he says,

> "Your throne, O *theos*, is forever and ever." (Heb. 1:8)

At first glance, the original psalm seems to be speaking about an Israelite king and thus could be using the lesser form of "god" (Heb. *elohim*, Gk. *theos*) as an honorary way of addressing him. Regardless of whether that is true—opinions vary—it is clear what the author of Hebrews is doing as he interprets Psalm 45. He is saying that the Father is addressing his Son specifically as "God" (*theos*) and ascribing to him eternal dominion.

1 John 5:19–20

Another instance where grammar matters is 1 John 5:19–20. The apostle John describes someone as both "the true God" and "eternal life." But at first blush it may seem unclear to whom he is referring. Let me provide a wooden translation:

> We know that we are from **God**. . . . And we know that the **Son** of God has come and given us a mind that we might know the truth, and we are in the one who is true, in his **Son** Jesus Christ. **This one** is the true *theos* and eternal life. (1 John 5:19–20)

The last sentence in 5:20 is our focus. John says that "this one" (Gk. *houtos*) is *theos*. But to whom does this demonstrative pronoun refer? There are two options, which I have set in bold: "God" (the Father) in 5:19 or the "Son" (2x) in 5:20.

Some argue that it must refer to "God" (the Father) in 5:19, which is grammatically possible. Three considerations, however, suggest otherwise. (1) In the vast majority of instances, the item that is nearer to the pronoun is the antecedent, rather than the one that is farther away; in this case, "Son" appears twice in a closer position to "this one" than does "God" (which is in a prior verse altogether). (2) Throughout the Gospel and first epistle of John, Jesus is often called both "true"/"truth" and "life."[2] In fact, *in this very verse* Jesus is called "the one who is true." While God (the Father) is also called "true" in John's Gospel,[3] it is more likely that "true" and "life" in 5:20 point to Jesus. (3) In John's writings the demonstrative pronoun "this one" (Gk. *houtos*) is regularly used in significant ways to refer to Jesus (e.g., John 1:2, 30; 4:29; 6:14, 42, 46), but it is rarely used to refer to the Father. Thus, the cumulative evidence suggests that John is referring to Jesus as "true *theos* and eternal life."

John 1:1; 10:33; and 20:28

Speaking of the apostle John, let me wrap up this section with three of the famous statements in his Gospel.

The first verse has received enormous attention, as well it should. Here is a wooden way of presenting it, which attempts to match the Greek word order:

> In the beginning was the Word,
> and the Word was in the presence of **the** *theos*,
> and *theos* was **the** Word. (John 1:1)

Our focus is on the last clause, which deals with *theos* and "Word," the latter of which refers to Jesus (1:14–17). The phrase is structured as a predicate nominative, where two nouns—that is, *theos* and "Word"—are linked up with each other using the verb *to be* (here, "was"). Importantly, in this instance the first noun (*theos*) does not have the article "the" (Gk. *ho*), while the second one ("Word") does. Since John does not put the article before *theos*, some, such as Jehovah's

---

2. E.g., John 1:4, 17; 5:26; 6:35, 51, 55; 7:18; 11:25; 14:6; 1 John 1:1–2; 5:11.
3. E.g., John 3:33; 5:26; 8:26.

Witnesses, argue that we should understand it as "a god"—that is, a vaguely divine being of some sort.

The problem is that Greek does not play by these rules. The absence of "the" does not mean we automatically insert "a" in English; Greek does not, strictly speaking, have an explicit "a" (indefinite article) anyhow. So one must think about it differently.

On close examination, John has made, *in Greek*, a rather brilliant move that easily gets lost in the translation. All the other options on the table (e.g., adding "the" before *theos*, removing "the" from before "Word," or reversing the order so that "Word" precedes *theos* in the clause) might result in distortions, such as collapsing all of *theos* into "Word" and leaving no space for Father or Spirit. John has worded it precisely to avoid such problems. Let me explain how.

Predicate nominatives basically convey A = B, and two rules come into play. First, if only one of the items has "the," that one logically fills the A slot and the other fills the B slot, regardless of the word order. Thus, in this case "the Word" fills A. The last clause in 1:1 is saying, "The Word was B"— even though the Greek word order is the other way around. Second, the same *theos* in the third clause has already appeared with "the" in the immediately preceding clause: "in the presence of **the** *theos*."[4] This makes clear that *theos* is definite: *the* God, not *a* god. In such situations it is quite common (but not mandatory) for "the" to be left out, if, as in the third clause here, its noun comes before the verb "to be." Consequently, what fills the B slot is not "a god" but clearly a reference to "**the** *theos*," even if "the" is not present.

What, then, does John accomplish by dropping this optional "the" before *theos* in the last clause? In effect, the one to whom

---

4. The practice of not translating this "the" is simply a matter of English, not Greek, style.

we are referring when we speak of the true *theos*—the Word is rightly understood as *that* being. A more clunky way of translating it would be, "The Word was that which *theos* was." The Word is of the same class, the same quality, as that of *theos*. As a result, it is certain that John is stating clearly—and quite delicately—that Jesus Christ, the Word, is fully "God." But by wording it the way he has, John maintains the distinction between the Word and "the" God that he already established in the second clause of the verse.

Later in the Gospel, John records an interesting accusation by the Jewish authorities: "We are not going to stone you for a good deed but for blasphemy, for you, being a man, make yourself [**the**] *theos*" (10:33). Regardless of whether they fully understand, let alone accept by faith, what Jesus is saying and doing, the opponents of Jesus clearly have deduced that he is making claims that extend far beyond what is true of prophets or even earthly messiahs. He has equated himself with *theos*, which is why they charge him with blasphemy. Interestingly, an early manuscript of John (papyrus 66) inserts the article "the" before *theos* (shown in brackets above), further amplifying the claim to divinity.

Granted, in the subsequent conversation, Jesus appears to deflect their accusation by pointing out that *theos* is used in Psalm 82 for angelic figures. But when you look at it closely, he is not denying divine status. Rather, he is shrewdly arguing that since it is not blasphemy to use *theos* for such angels, surely it is not blasphemy to refer to the truly divine Son as *theos* as well. He concludes by solidifying their very accusation: "I am in the Father, and the Father is in me" (10:38).

Finally, we come to the poignant scene with "doubting" Thomas. After Jesus patiently shows Thomas his wounds, John records that "Thomas answered and said to him, 'My Lord and my *theos*!'" (20:28). The formerly troubled disciple is now able confidently to confess his faith. The direct addressee of Thomas's words is "him," such that Thomas aims "my Lord and my *theos*" at one and the same person (not two people)—namely, Jesus. And, to revisit chapter 3, Thomas draws on both Lord/ *kyrios* and *theos* to refer to Jesus. It is a fitting end to what was started in John 1:1.

In sum, there is no reason to doubt that these seven passages, distributed across multiple New Testament authors, directly call Jesus *theos*.

Five Debated Instances

Let me now briefly survey five other instances where it is possible that Jesus is called *theos* but where some sticky debate remains.[5] (Note: all biblical translations in this section are my own.)

John 1:18

In the famous passage John 1:18, John writes, "No one has ever seen *theos*; the only _____, the one who is at the Father's side, has made him known." I covered this passage briefly in chapter 3, as it features the Greek term *monogenēs* ("only" or "only begotten"). The focus here is on the subsequent word. The vast majority of manuscripts put "Son" in the blank, while only a handful put "God." From a scribal perspective, the difference would have been small, for the words would have been abbreviated ΥΣ versus ΘΣ. And arguments for or against each of them are indecisive. So it is hard to be definitive about what John actually wrote. At a minimum, a few early Christian scribes clearly thought it was okay to read "God" there in reference to Jesus.

---

5. To this list could be added the disputed contenders for the Granville Sharp Rule listed above: Eph. 5:5; 2 Thess. 1:12; 1 Tim. 5:21; 2 Tim. 4:1.

Acts 20:28

Acts 20:28 is another tricky verse that involves a few issues. Some manuscripts read, "church of the *theos*, which he bought with his own blood." Others add "Lord and" between "the" and *theos*. If this longer version is correct, then the passage is clearly describing Jesus as both "**the** Lord and *theos*," making this very similar to Titus 2:13 and 2 Peter 1:1 (see p. 108 above). But other issues arise with the last few words (Gk. *tou haimatos tou idiou*). If they should be read, "his own blood," then Jesus must be in view since the Father does not have literal blood. But if they should be read, "the blood of his own," then "his" refers to Father, and "own" refers to Jesus. The evidence could go either way, so we are left hanging. This verse *may* be referring to Jesus as *theos*, but that reading of it is not a slam dunk.

Galatians 2:20

Yet another scribal issue is found in Galatians 2:20. The basic sentence is this: "I live by faith in the _____ who loved me." Some very good manuscripts read, "Son of God," in the blank. But other very good ones read, "*theos* and Christ."[6] In the latter case, we are once more back in a situation where the one article "the" applies to both *theos* and "Christ." It is difficult to be fully certain what Paul indeed wrote. At a minimum a large number of early Christian scribes transmitted a text that does clearly call Jesus *theos*.

1 Timothy 3:16

Though I discussed 1 Timothy 3:16 in chapter 1, it is worth another look because of its well-known scribal variation.

---

6. A similar scribal reading is found in Jude 5, where papyrus 72 reads neither "Lord" nor "God" nor "Jesus" (as with most of the other alternatives) but, somewhat surprisingly, "God Christ" (Gk. *theos christos*).

While many manuscripts read, "Who was manifested in the flesh," many others read, "*Theos* was manifested in the flesh" (e.g., the KJV reads, "God was manifest in the flesh"). The difference in Greek is very slight: "who" would be written ΟΣ, while *theos* would be abbreviated ΘΣ. Only one small stroke distinguishes them, and arguments are once again balanced as to which reading most likely originated with Paul. Either way, a large number of early Christians used "*Theos* was manifested," clearly accepting Jesus as "God."

Romans 9:5

Perhaps the most interesting and complex passage is Romans 9:5, for it comes at the heart of Paul's magisterial epistle to Rome and does not involve a textual variant (as the other four passages do). Rather, the issue boils down to punctuation: Where does Paul intend commas and periods? Early manuscripts do not always include such markings. Usually that poses no issue, as context makes it clear. But in this case, punctuation makes a huge difference. There are basically four options (each of which requires a slightly different wording in English, though in Greek it is the same):

. . . the Christ. *Theos* who is over all be blessed forever.

. . . the Christ who is over all. *Theos* be blessed forever.

. . . the Christ, who is over all, *theos* blessed forever.

. . . the Christ, the one who is, as *theos* over all, blessed forever.

The first two place a period between "Christ" and *theos*, such that they are firmly distinguished. The third and fourth place a comma between "Christ" and *theos*, such that they refer to the same person. Good arguments can be made for each, which is why there has been no settled opinion.[7]

In short, there are five intriguing instances where the needle could point either way, depending on how one assesses the textual or grammatical evidence. The fact that there are seven solid ones, however, at least demonstrates that there is no dogmatic reason why any of these others should be excluded out of the gate.

Other Designations

The New Testament does not stop with *theos*. Other words or phrases are used for Jesus that, when understood in light of the rest of the New Testament, supplement the evidence of this chapter. Prior to his birth, he is called "Immanuel," translated as "God with us" (Matt. 1:23; citing Isa. 7:14). It is debated whether this instance of referring to Jesus as "*theos* with us" is the same thing as calling him *theos* directly, for it could simply be a poetic way of describing how he manifests the love or presence of God with his people. But in light of the emphasis placed on Jesus's supernatural conception in Matthew's birth account, it is more likely that the evangelist is making the much stronger claim with "Immanuel."

Jesus is also called "the wisdom of God" (1 Cor. 1:24), "the glory of the Lord" (2 Cor. 3:18), and "the image of God" (2 Cor. 4:4). Finally, Paul writes that "in him all the fullness of deity [Gk. *theotēs*] dwells bodily" (Col. 2:9, my trans.; cf. 1:19). Paul here uses a derivative form of *theos* to describe how Jesus in some mysterious way contains the entire fullness of what it means for God to be "God"—indeed, we could render *theotēs* as "Godness"—in his very body.

---

7. That said, I believe the fourth option deserves more attention, as it makes arguably the clearest sense of the Greek.

Summary

In this chapter, I have examined several specific passages where it is sometimes possible and sometimes certain that Jesus is called *theos* by a New Testament author, along with a handful of other phrases that connote the same idea. Given all the other evidence put forth in the preceding chapters, it seems unavoidable to conclude the following: What the early Christians mean by calling him *theos* is not that he is an angel, "a god," or nebulously "divine," but that Jesus Christ is of the same essence as *theos*. What God is, Jesus is, such that he can even be called *theos* in the same way.

So What?

The material in this chapter requires us to roll up our sleeves and get our hands dirty in some details of Greek grammar and textual variants. This may be taxing for some readers, but if nothing else, these passages reveal the need to take the task of reading Scripture closely, word for word, for all its worth. Precision matters for doctrine, and doctrine matters for life.

But given the intricacies involved, attempting to argue with a Jehovah's Witness on your front porch about the nuances of "the" in John 1:1 or the punctuation of Romans 9:5 is probably going to be unproductive. Given their skepticism toward any Bible that is not the New World Translation, you may make better headway in other passages, such as Mark 1:1 (see chap. 3), where even their translation corroborates how the New Testament teaches that Jesus is fully God, not "a god."

Conclusion

We have covered a lot of ground in this short volume, as I have probed numerous angles of the question "Does the Bible teach that Jesus is truly God?" I have attempted not only to show *that* the New Testament answers yes but also to marshal all the evidence for *how* it renders that answer:

1. He was preexistent before his human birth, such that he had a real, spiritual existence in heaven, before he "came" or "was sent" to earth.
2. He stands in a unique relationship of "Son" to the heavenly Father. This sonship transcends what was commonly said about kings/messiahs in the ancient world; it defines the relation of Son to Father as one of eternal begetting.
3. He is called Lord/*kyrios* in a way that adopts the Jewish treatment of the divine name YHWH. As a result, he is the subject of fascinating rereadings of the Old Testament by the early Christians. Namely, key passages, prerogatives, and metaphors that in the Old Testament were used of God himself are fully revealed to incorporate the Son. He is (and has always been) the God of Israel *as Son*.
4. He not only *intercedes in* but is the direct *recipient of* actual religious worship (prayers, singing, etc.) from the earliest days—perhaps even during his earthly ministry.

5. He stands in a complex relationship with the Father and the Holy Spirit, such that his divine being is revealed to be fully *Trinitarian*.
6. He is directly called *theos* ("God") and other exalted terms at various points in the New Testament.

This evidence by itself establishes the answer to the question driving this book. Yet some readers may be asking, What about the other key passages that have not been addressed here?

Indeed, I have saved the best for last. Four passages bring everything together, especially as they combine elements of the preceding chapters: preexistence, divine sonship, use of the Old Testament, divine prerogatives, worship, and so on. I briefly survey them and demonstrate how they not only convey the highest possible "divine Christology" but—bringing us full circle—marry it to "human Christology" at the same time. In other words, these key passages undergird both Nicaea and Chalcedon by serving as the best "one-stop shops" in the New Testament on the full humanity *and* full divinity of Jesus Christ.

Philippians 2:6–11

In Philippians 2:6–11, a pivotal section in this epistle, Paul begins by articulating in no uncertain terms the full divinity of Jesus Christ. He "was in the form" (Gk. *morphē*) of God and "equal" (Gk. *isa*) to God: that is, from his preexistence the Son shares the nature or essence of God and is his equal (Phil. 2:6). He did not, however, cling to this exalted status but took on the form of a servant and the likeness of humans (2:7–8).[1]

---

1. A challenging clause appears in Phil. 2:7: "He emptied himself." Some argue that the verb (Gk. *ekenōsen*) means that Jesus somehow dedivinized himself (the so-called "kenosis" theory), such that he became "ungod" when he took on human flesh. But a close analysis indicates that he "emptied" himself not by subtracting his divinity but by adding flesh. For a time on earth, Jesus denied himself the full expression of his divine essence by assuming full humanity, such that he hungered, thirsted, slept, etc. But as we

This humiliation culminates when Jesus becomes "obedient to the point of death" on a cross (2:8). But upon his resurrection and ascension, the Son of God is exalted to the heavenly throne once more (2:9). Here Paul gives two linchpins of the full divinity of Jesus. First, he is bestowed with the "name above all names" (my trans.). While the name itself is likely Lord/*kyrios* (2:11), it is just as important to see that possessing this all-high name is something that is true only of God in the Old Testament (e.g., Neh. 9:5; Pss. 138:2; 148:13). Second, Paul applies a YHWH passage from the Old Testament to Jesus in Philippians 2:10–11 when he writes, "At the name of Jesus every knee should bow . . . and every tongue confess . . . ." This language is taken directly from Isaiah 45:23, where YHWH declares that *to himself* "every knee will bow and tongue confess" (my trans.). Thus, the worship that is to be offered to YHWH by all people in the world (per Isa. 45) is now to be offered to Jesus, whom we are to confess as Lord/*kyrios* (Phil. 2:11).

In these verses Paul could hardly express any more clearly that Jesus Christ was and is divine in the fullest sense but also fully human, winning salvation for us in the flesh on the cross. The arc of Christ is clear: (1) exaltation (in his preexistence) → (2) humiliation (in his incarnation and death) → (3) exaltation (in his resurrection and ascension).[2] The final step is very important Christologically: death could not hold Jesus if he is indeed divine.

It is worth noting that many scholars argue that this section may have been an early Christian confession that was already in circulation before Paul adopted it in his epistle. If so, the

---

have already seen, he retained all his divinity even as he clothed himself in a body. His self-emptying is, in effect, subtraction by addition.

2. The same arc lies behind Jesus's prayer in John 17:5, as he is anticipating his impending death: "Father, glorify me in your own presence with the glory that I had with you before the world existed."

roots of this high confession of Jesus as the God-man go back very early.

Colossians 1:15–20

Paul provides another angle on his high Christology in Colossians 1:15–20, a famous passage that also may go back to an earlier period in the church. He describes the Son of God as the "image [Gk. *eikōn*] of the invisible God" and the "firstborn" (Gk. *prōtotokos*)—that is, the preeminent one—over all creation (1:15). To avoid the possible misinterpretation that "firstborn" means Jesus is merely a created being, Paul goes on to say that this same Son is the one who created "all things" in heaven and on earth (1:16) and that he was "before all things" (1:17). These are extremely significant statements declaring that the Son was preexistent before the creation of all things *and* that he is the one who created, borrowing "heaven" and "earth" language precisely from Genesis 1. He could not be a creature if he created "all things." Moreover, Paul describes how the Son exercises total sovereignty over all creation—an exclusive divine prerogative—when he says that "in him all things hold together" (1:17). Such statements surely could not be made about mere humans.

Yet Paul does not leave us gasping in the thin air of cosmic eternity. He goes on to describe how this same preexistent and creating Son died and was resurrected (1:18), so that, in the mysterious way we described in chapter 4, he might incorporate the entire church across time and place as his "body" (1:18).

Paul then summarizes by reiterating Jesus's full divinity ("in him all the fullness was pleased to dwell," 1:19, my trans.) *and* full humanity ("making peace by the blood of his cross," 1:20). The arc of Colossians 1:15–20 is thus the same as that in Philippians 2 but with different phrasing. The preexistent one, who is divine Creator and Sustainer, also took on flesh to reconcile man to God by his death. In fact, this is a pretty good summary of the entire Christian gospel.

Hebrews 1:1–4

Shifting to Hebrews, we find that the author traces the same exaltation-humiliation-exaltation arc. He identifies Jesus Christ as the preeminent "Son" and Creator of the entire world (Heb. 1:2). He then describes how this Son is the "radiance" (Gk. *apaugasma*) of the glory of God as well as the "imprint" or "stamp" or "mark" (Gk. *charaktēr*) of God's very being (1:3). The exact meaning of this language is wonderfully hard to pin down,[3] but one thing is clear: the author is striving to describe how the Son can be distinct from the Father but share in the one divine essence.

The writer goes on to say not only that this Son is the Creator and exists as the imprint of God but that he also "upholds all things" by the mere word of his power (1:3, my trans.), yet again reflecting the exclusive sovereignty of the Godhead over "all things." All that said, this same divine Son made "purification for sins" in the flesh (1:3). And, as with Philippians and Colossians, he is exalted once more to the right hand of God (Heb. 1:3), inheriting a name superior to even that of angels (1:4). After his humiliation, the Son is exalted to his rightful position in heaven.

John 1:1–18

We make our way at last to the place where this book started: John 1. Though I have touched on it briefly in other chapters, it can now be examined in more detail. The hope is that John 1 can now be seen not as some kind of innovative outlier but as

---

3. A similar use of "radiance" is found in Wis. 7:26, describing how God's "wisdom" (Gk. *sophia*) is his "radiance" (Gk. *apaugasma*).

the best crystallization of what the New Testament otherwise teaches over and over again. In other words, the divine Christ of John 1 is not an inventive idea that appears in John's head alone, but rather, it echoes what can be found elsewhere in Paul, Peter, the Synoptics, Hebrews, and so on.

John begins with the preexistence of the Son of God: "In the beginning was the Word" (1:1). This statement draws on the language of Genesis 1:1 to make clear that when God moved to create the world "in the beginning," the Son already existed. He did not come to be but always "was." John clarifies this point by saying that the "Word" was "in the presence of [Gk. *pros*]" God (my trans.)—and, as covered in chapter 6, John goes on to say that this "Word" indeed is fully *theos*.

But why does John use "Word"? He is almost certainly drawing on Genesis itself. For if you examine Genesis 1–2 closely, you find that the means by which God creates is *speaking*. He does not use tools or raw materials, but he merely speaks, and things come to be. This speech-act of God in Genesis is now revealed by John *to be the very second person of the Godhead*, otherwise known as the Son. And if you look back at Genesis 1:2, you find that the third divine person, the Holy Spirit, is present too. John is remixing all this to make clear what was veiled in Genesis. The creation of all things is a fully triune act, yet the active cause of creation *is the speaking of God*. Thus, John can conclude that "all things" were made through the Word (John 1:3).

Then a stunning thing happens: this "Word"—this God the Son, who existed before creation and actually created all things as the speech-act of the Godhead—this very *theos* "became flesh" and "dwelt among us" (1:14). This is the incarnation of the preincarnate God. Fully God: *made flesh*.[4]

---

4. In a parenthetical aside (John 1:15), John the Baptist declares this Jesus to be superior to him because he was "before" (Gk. *prōtos*) him in time—perhaps alluding to the Son's preexistence.

To wrap things up, then, the apostle brings the divine and human aspects together by stating that the Son of God "has explained" (or "made known") the invisible God (1:18, my trans.). The enfleshing of God as Jesus Christ is how God has been unveiled, expounded, explained, or manifested to the world. That, in short, is what the orthodox teaching of the church has been all along, as eventually expressed in the creeds. And it comes directly from Scripture.

So, yes, John 1 is a great place to go to prove the divinity of Jesus.

Closing Thoughts

What is it that made the early Christians draw the conclusion that their friend and rabbi—this human Jesus with whom they had walked, dined, and traveled—was indeed fully God in every sense of the word? And what led them to take the step of worshiping him as such?

Perhaps it was their witnessing of his miracles (John 10:38; 14:11).[5] Perhaps it was their postresurrection encounter with him. Perhaps it was the variety of ways he directly or indirectly declared his divine identity during his ministry. Perhaps it was their transformed understanding of Israel's Scriptures. Perhaps it was God himself, who even called his Son "God" (Heb. 1:8; cf. Ps. 45:6). It was likely a combination of all the above.

But however they got there, what makes this phenomenon perhaps most intriguing is this: the New Testament never really argues in detail for the divinity of Jesus. Nowhere do we find

---

5. I have intentionally avoided placing Christ's miraculous deeds front and center in this discussion. On the one hand, Jesus does, in John 10:38 and 14:11, affirm that his miraculous "works" display his closeness to the Father. On the other hand, numerous nondivine persons in the Old and New Testaments—including Moses, Elijah, Elisha, Peter, and so on—do miraculous things. Miracles can thus simply convey that God is at work, not that a divine being is directly doing them. Most of the miracles of Jesus, then, certainly prove that he is a prophet (Luke 7:16), but in isolation, they are not necessarily the clearest places to go specifically to argue for his full divinity.

a long treatise where Paul or John or anyone else is specifically trying to prove in any elaborate way that Jesus is fully man and fully God. The closest we come are the four passages summarized above, but even they are not *arguing* or *defending* the position. They are simply elaborating on its implications.[6]

For many, this is a big problem, for they want to find a key passage in the New Testament that decisively proves the case for the divinity of Jesus. The lack of an explicit argument, however, is perhaps the best argument of all. The New Testament authors did not feel the need to defend or prove the idea that Jesus is God. *They assumed it.* It was the inescapable conclusion toward which they were all drawn. This confession of the full lordship and the full divine status of Jesus Christ exploded overnight and was shared by all Christians. It shows up everywhere in the New Testament, even in places one might not expect. It was the air they breathed.

Thus, the earliest Christology is not that Jesus was a man and got upgraded. The earliest Christology is not that Jesus was an angelic spirit being who shifted into human form. The earliest Christology is the highest and lowest and everything between: in Jesus Christ is found all the fullness of God bodily. The man Jesus is truly God.

---

6. For instance, the crystal-clear teaching on the deity of Jesus in Phil. 2:6–11 is actually aimed at exhorting the Christians at Philippi to pursue greater humility toward one another (2:1–5). Even the majesty of John 1:1–18 is aimed at reassuring Christians about God's love expressed in making them "children of God" (1:12).

Selected Bibliography

Bates, Matthew W. *The Birth of the Trinity: Jesus, God, and Spirit in New Testament and Early Christian Interpretations of the Old Testament.* Oxford: Oxford University Press, 2015.

Bauckham, Richard J. *Jesus and the God of Israel: God Crucified and Other Studies on the New Testament's Christology of Divine Identity.* Grand Rapids, MI: Eerdmans, 2008.

Bauckham, Richard J. "The Throne of God and the Worship of Jesus." In *The Jewish Roots of Christological Monotheism: Papers from the St. Andrews Conference on the Historical Origins of the Worship of Jesus,* edited by Cary C. Newman, James R. Davila, and Gladys S. Lewis, 43–69. Supplements to the Journal for the Study of Judaism 63. Leiden: Brill, 1999.

Bird, Michael F. *Are You the One Who Is to Come? The Historical Jesus and the Messianic Question.* Grand Rapids, MI: Baker Academic, 2009.

Bird, Michael F. *Jesus the Eternal Son: Answering Adoptionistic Christology.* Grand Rapids, MI: Eerdmans, 2017.

Bird, Michael F., Craig A. Evans, Simon J. Gathercole, Charles E. Hill, and Chris Tilling. *How God Became Jesus: The Real Origins of Belief in Jesus' Divine Nature; A Response to Bart D. Ehrman.* Grand Rapids, MI: Zondervan, 2014.

Bullard, Collin. *Jesus and the Thoughts of Many Hearts: Implicit Christology and Jesus' Knowledge in the Gospel of Luke*. Library of New Testament Studies 530. London: T&T Clark, 2015.

Capes, David B. *The Divine Christ: Paul, the Lord Jesus, and the Scriptures of Israel*. Grand Rapids, MI: Baker Academic, 2018.

Carrell, Peter. *Jesus and the Angels: Angelology and the Christology of the Apocalypse of John*. Society for New Testament Studies Monograph Series 95. Cambridge: Cambridge University Press, 2005.

Collins, Adela Yarbro, and John J. Collins. *King and Messiah as Son of God: Divine, Human, and Angelic Messianic Figures in Biblical and Related Literature*. Grand Rapids, MI: Eerdmans, 2008.

Crowe, Brandon D., and Carl R. Trueman, eds. *The Essential Trinity: New Testament Foundations and Practical Relevance*. Phillipsburg, NJ: P&R, 2017.

Fee, Gordon. *Pauline Christology: An Exegetical-Theological Study*. Peabody, MA: Hendrickson, 2007.

Gathercole, Simon J. *The Preexistent Son: Recovering the Christologies of Matthew, Mark, and Luke*. Grand Rapids, MI: Eerdmans, 2006.

Gieschen, Charles A. *Angelomorphic Christology: Antecedents and Early Evidence*. Arbeiten zur Geschichte des antiken Judentums und des Urchristentums 42. Leiden: Brill, 1998.

Grindheim, Sigurd. *God's Equal: What Can We Know about Jesus' Self-Understanding in the Synoptic Gospels*. Library of New Testament Studies 446. London: T&T Clark, 2011.

Hays, Richard B. *Echoes of Scripture in the Gospels*. Waco, TX: Baylor University Press, 2016.

Hengel, Martin. *Between Jesus and Paul: Studies in the Earliest History of Christianity*. Translated by John Bowden. London: SCM, 1983.

Hengel, Martin. *Studies in Early Christology.* Edinburgh: T&T Clark, 1995.

Henrichs-Tarasenkova, Nina. *Luke's Christology of Divine Identity.* Library of New Testament Studies 224. London: T&T Clark, 2015.

Hill, Wesley. *Paul and the Trinity: Persons, Relations, and the Pauline Letters.* Grand Rapids, MI: Eerdmans, 2015.

Hurtado, Larry W. *Honoring the Son: Jesus in Earliest Christian Devotional Practice.* Bellingham, WA: Lexham, 2018.

Hurtado, Larry W. *How on Earth Did Jesus Become a God? Historical Questions about Earliest Devotion to Jesus.* Grand Rapids, MI: Eerdmans, 2005.

Hurtado, Larry W. *Lord Jesus Christ: Devotion to Jesus in Earliest Christianity.* Grand Rapids, MI: Eerdmans, 2003.

Hurtado, Larry W. *One God, One Lord: Early Christian Devotion and Ancient Jewish Monotheism.* London: SCM, 1988.

Irons, Charles Lee. "A Lexical Defense of the Johannine 'Only-Begotten.'" In *Retrieving Eternal Generation*, edited by Fred Sanders and Scott R. Swain, 98–116. Grand Rapids, MI: Zondervan, 2017.

Köstenberger, Andreas J., and Scott R. Swain. *Father, Son and Spirit: The Trinity and John's Gospel.* New Studies in Biblical Theology 24. Downers Grove, IL: InterVarsity Press, 2008.

Lanier, Gregory R. "Luke's Distinctive Use of the Temple: Portraying the Divine Visitation." *Journal of Theological Studies* 65, no. 2 (2014): 433–62.

Lanier, Gregory R. *Old Testament Conceptual Metaphors and the Christology of Luke's Gospel.* Library of New Testament Studies 591. London: T&T Clark, 2018.

Lee, Aquila H. I. *From Messiah to Preexistent Son: Jesus' Self-Consciousness and Early Christian Exegesis of Messianic Psalms.* Wissenschaftliche Untersuchungen zum Neuen Testament, 2nd ser., vol. 192. Tübingen: Mohr Siebeck, 2005.

Lozano, Ray M. *The* Proskynesis *of Jesus in the New Testament: A Study on the Significance of Jesus as an Object of* προσκυνέω *in the New Testament Writings*. Library of New Testament Studies 609. London: T&T Clark, 2020.

Macaskill, Grant. *Revealed Wisdom and Inaugurated Eschatology in Ancient Judaism and Early Christianity*. Supplements to the Journal for the Study of Judaism 115. Leiden: Brill, 2007.

McCready, Douglas. *He Came Down from Heaven: The Preexistence of Christ and the Christian Faith*. Downers Grove, IL: InterVarsity Press, 2005.

Müller, Mogens. *The Expression "Son of Man" and the Development of Christology: A History of Interpretation*. New York: Routledge, 2014.

Peppard, Michael. *The Son of God in the Roman World: Divine Sonship in Its Social and Political Context*. Oxford: Oxford University Press, 2011.

Rowe, C. Kavin. *Early Narrative Christology: The Lord in the Gospel of Luke*. Beihefte zur Zeitschrift für die neutestamentliche Wissenschaft 139. Berlin: de Gruyter, 2006.

Scott, Matthew. *The Hermeneutics of Christological Psalmody in Paul: An Intertextual Enquiry*. Society for New Testament Studies Monograph Series 158. Cambridge: Cambridge University Press, 2014.

Stuckenbruck, Loren. *Angel Veneration and Christology: A Study in Early Judaism and in the Christology of the Apocalypse of John*. Wissenschaftliche Untersuchungen zum Neuen Testament, 2nd ser., vol. 70. Tübingen: Mohr Siebeck, 1995.

Tait, Michael. *Jesus, the Divine Bridegroom, in Mark 2:11–22: Mark's Christology Upgraded*. Analecta Biblica 185. Roma: Gregorian and Biblical Press, 2010.

Tilling, Chris. *Paul's Divine Christology*. Grand Rapids, MI: Eerdmans, 2015.

Waaler, Erik. *The Shema and the First Commandment in First Co-rinthians: An Intertextual Approach to Paul's Re-Reading of Deuteronomy.* Wissenschaftliche Untersuchungen zum Neuen Testament, 2nd ser., vol. 253. Tübingen: Mohr Siebeck, 2008.

General Index

Scripture Index